THE ART OF INTERACTIVE TEACHING

"*The Art of Interactive Teaching* gives a road map to teachers, curriculum specialists, and administrators who want classroom lessons to be ways of getting students involved in content-driven ideas and grasping issues that have no easy, crisp answers. This book comes at a time when more and more reformers, practitioners, and researchers are seeking sources for such forms of student-centered teaching at all levels of schooling. It nicely encapsulates years of work on using prompts to get at big ideas, leading discussions that discourage yes-no answers, and getting students to think well behind what conventional teaching allows. Selma Wassermann brings expertise, credibility, and clear prose in laying out how interactive teaching can occur in classrooms."
—*Larry Cuban, Professor Emeritus of Education, Stanford University, USA*

In this book, Selma Wassermann, international expert on classroom interactions, sets the stage for the relevance of the interactive teaching method, provides data and classroom examples that support its effectiveness at all student learning levels and in different subject areas, and offers detailed and specific help for teachers who are considering embarking on this approach to teaching. Coverage includes "teaching to the big ideas," preparing students, and the basics of developing good listening, responding, and questioning skills in an interactive discussion. A chapter on learning to become reflective practitioners deals with how teachers may become more aware of what they are saying and in better control of framing responses and questions in the art of interactive teaching. The book draws from the author's long experience and study of interactive teaching using the case method rooted in the Harvard Business School's approach to large class instruction.

Selma Wassermann is Professor Emerita, Faculty of Education, Simon Fraser University, Canada.

THE ART OF INTERACTIVE TEACHING

Listening, Responding, Questioning

Selma Wassermann

NEW YORK AND LONDON

First published 2017
by Routledge
711 Third Avenue, New York, NY 10017

and by Routledge
2 Park Square, Milton Park, Abingdon, Oxon, OX14 4RN

Routledge is an imprint of the Taylor & Francis Group, an informa business

© 2017 Taylor & Francis

The right of Selma Wassermann to be identified as author of this work has been asserted by her in accordance with sections 77 and 78 of the Copyright, Designs and Patents Act 1988.

All rights reserved. No part of this book may be reprinted or reproduced or utilised in any form or by any electronic, mechanical, or other means, now known or hereafter invented, including photocopying and recording, or in any information storage or retrieval system, without permission in writing from the publishers.

Trademark notice: Product or corporate names may be trademarks or registered trademarks, and are used only for identification and explanation without intent to infringe.

Library of Congress Cataloging in Publication Data
Names: Wassermann, Selma, author.
Title: The art of interactive teaching : listening, responding, questioning / Selma Wassermann.
Description: New York : Routledge, [2017] | Includes bibliographical references and index.
Identifiers: LCCN 2016057304| ISBN 9781138041165 (hardback) | ISBN 9781138041172 (pbk.) | ISBN 9781315174624 (EISBN)
Subjects: LCSH: Interaction analysis in education. | Communication in education. | Discussion. | Classroom environment. | Effective teaching. | Teacher-student relationships.
Classification: LCC LB1034 .W376 2017 | DDC 371.102/2—dc23
LC record available at https://lccn.loc.gov/2016057304

ISBN: 978-1-138-04116-5 (hbk)
ISBN: 978-1-138-04117-2 (pbk)
ISBN: 978-1-315-17462-4 (ebk)

Typeset in Bembo
by diacriTech, Chennai

For my adorable greats, Maya, Kai and one more to come.

CONTENTS

Preface xi
Acknowledgments xv

1 **Interactive Teaching: The What, the Why, and the How** 1
   Class Discussions and Class Discussions 3
   Interactive Teaching – It's Not for Every Teacher 6
   Choosing Interactive Teaching 8
   References 8

2 **The Shape of Teaching and Learning in the Interactive Classroom** 9
   What's the Big Idea? 9
   Searching for the Meaning of Big Ideas 11
   Big Ideas Lead to the Generation of a Curriculum Task
      or Investigation 13
   Small Group Work 14
   Follow-up Studies 15
   How Long, Oh, How Long? 16
   References 16

3 **Preparing for Interactive Teaching** 17
   Tolerating Dissonance 17
   Maintaining and Relinquishing Control 19
   Knowing your Own Style 20
   Establishing the Contract 21
   References 25

4 Scenes from Interactive Classrooms — 26
The Train 26
Germs Make Me Sick! 31
The Hockey Card 33
Notes 36
References 36

5 Basic Interactive Skills: Listening, Attending, Apprehending, Making Meaning — 37
Now the Fun Begins 40
A Personal Training Program for Improving One's Listening and Attending Skills 40
Practice Tasks in Listening, Attending, Paraphrasing, and Being Non-Judgmental 42
Postgame Reflections on Simulations 42
Conclusion 43
References 43

6 Basic Interactive Skills: Responding, Saying Back, Paraphrasing, Interpreting — 44
Waiting for Students To Express their Ideas 45
Being Non-Judgmental in Accepting Students' Responses: Appreciating Students' Ideas 45
Conditions that Limit and Actually Crush Student Thinking 46
Becoming Aware of Differences in Responding 48
Self-assessment 50
References 51

7 Basic Interactive Skills: Questioning — 52
Unproductive Questions 54
Less-than-Productive Questions 58
Productive Questions 60
Guidelines for Productive Questions 61
Conclusion 66
Note 67
References 67

8 The Well-Orchestrated Discussion — 68

9   Reflecting in Action   78
It's Eezier with a Buddy   80
References   81

Appendix A: Practice in Listening, Attending, Paraphrasing, and Being Non-Judgmental   82
Introduction   82
Suggested Practice Statements of Teachers Talking to Teachers   83
More Suggested Practice Statements of Student Teachers
  Talking to Teachers   84
Thirteen More Suggested Practice Statements of Teachers Being
  Introduced to Discussion Teaching   86
A Dozen More Practice Statements Made by Younger Students
  and Overheard in Real Classrooms   87

Appendix B: Practice in Listening, Attending, and Responding   88
Set 1: Listening, Attending, and Responding with Paraphrasing   88
Set 2: Listening, Attending, and Responding with Paraphrasing
  and Interpreting   89
Now the Fun Begins   91
Set 3: More Practice in Attending and Paraphrasing, with the Added
  Dimension of Interpreting   91

Appendix C: Task Analysis   92

Appendix D: Analyzing Interactions   93

Appendix E: Cases   95
The Hockey Card   96
Germs are Germs   101
The Case of Barry   104

Index   *110*

PREFACE

The journey I've taken in becoming a "discussion leader" began during my early days as a graduate student at New York University, where I watched and studied Louis Raths interacting with his classes as he conducted discussions based on his theoretical work on thinking and valuing. This was the first time that I had witnessed "interactive teaching," having been subject to years of lectures in which the only chances students got to talk were when the teacher asked a question and one student was singled out to respond with the "right" answer. Raths's interactions were astonishing to me – putting us in situations in which we were asked for our ideas, to which he responded with what, at that time, we called "clarifying questions." It was the first time that I saw students being called on to offer ideas and to have them put under serious scrutiny with higher order questions. Student responses were never judged correct or incorrect; the door was left open for further thinking. The discussions were dynamic – and although this was a new teacher–student classroom scenario for most of us, it was thrilling and I began to mimic some of those responses and use higher order questions in my own work with students, however ineptly and clumsily, without any appreciation for what was actually coming out of my mouth. Losing the evaluative comments were a challenge – since by implicit and explicit teaching, that was my deeply reinforced experience with schools and teachers at all levels.

The second leg of my journey began with my introduction to the work of Ted Parsons, at the University of California, Berkeley, in 1971. Parsons developed what he called Guided Self-Analysis – a series of "grids" that asked teachers to examine and scrutinize the nature of their responses and questions in an interactive dialogue. Parsons's work was intended to provide teachers with the tools for examining their teacher–student interactions, with an eye toward improving their higher order questions and responses. Although I tried to use Parsons's "grids" with some of my graduate students, as they applied "teaching for thinking" to their classroom practice, I found, as they did, that the grids were too cumbersome and too time-consuming for teachers to use effectively. But for me, they were eye-openers into how responses and questions could be analyzed, giving me the first tools to begin to examine my own questions and responses more accurately.

At that time, the introduction of the use of videotapes to observe, in retrospect, teacher styles and interactions was an innovation that made it possible for teachers-in-training to study their own classroom strategies as they worked on their own professional development. My first experience with watching myself work with a group of Grade 6 students was deeply embarrassing. Although I was, by now, fully appreciative of what constituted higher order questions and "clarifying responses" in teacher–student discussions, I as yet had no way of tuning in to what I was actually saying. Nor did I realize that such reflection in action was a critical part of learning and developing effective interactive skills. Watching the videotape was a lesson in humility. I was able to use Parsons's grids to focus on the nature of my questions and responses, despite how unwieldy they were – and once I understood that not only the way the question was worded, but also tone of voice made a difference, I began to take more seriously the task of learning to listen to myself while at the same watching for the effect of my responses and questions on the subsequent responses of my students.

Redesigning Parsons's grids into a more easy-to-use single "Analysis Sheet" helped me with not only studies of my own classroom interactions, but gave me a more effective tool for use with my university students who were studying "teaching for thinking." And the task of teaching many students, both pre-service and in-service teachers, was a constant and continuing series of lessons for my own interactive teaching work – for as I have said in other contexts, my students have always been my best teachers.

The *pièce de rèsistance* of my journey was the singular experience of watching and studying Roland ("Chris") Christensen, at the Harvard Graduate School of Business, whom I consider to be the master of discussion teaching. The way he used questions and responses to dig into the minds of students was like watching and listening to Lang Lang perform the impossibly difficult Rachmaninoff Piano Concerto #3 – with fingers so nimble he made it look easy. But anyone who knows music knows that it is one of the most difficult piano pieces in the repertoire. Watching and listening to Christensen made it look easy – but only to the uninitiated. It did, however, spur me on to work more seriously and more intensively on my own discussion teaching interactions, with a more concerted effort on listening to self in action. More video feedback enabled this process and made me aware, also, that this journey of learning to listen and to observe the self in the act of interactive teaching is an ongoing journey – that one never reaches the terminus, that this kind of professional development goes on forever. It has been a long journey, but in my view, learning to become an interactive teacher has given me, by far, the most powerful teaching strategies I possess – the strategies that have the best chance for promoting the kinds of learning goals we say we want for all students.

As unintended consequences go, I never expected that becoming a discussion leader would change my behavior not only in class, but outside of class as well. For learning to listen, to respond to what has been said, to apprehend, and even to question, has permeated my life in other substantial ways. For once I had become more skilled in these interactions, I found that I became "that person" – i.e., the one who listens, apprehends, responds, questions – outside of school settings as well. To be able to apprehend that a checkout clerk at the supermarket might be tired or cranky or suffering from an overlong day and to respond with thoughtfulness and kindness makes these types of people-to-people interactions more human. And especially for those who are close to me and whom I love, learning to be a good, respectful, and non-judgmental listener had a payoff larger than Peru.

And for all of that I am immensely grateful.

For those teachers who are not daunted by such a journey, there are now better tools to learn the art of interactive teaching, thanks to the teachers who worked with me for many years, helping me with their feedback and their guidance to develop more sophisticated practice tasks and task analysis tools that can aid other teachers in learning these techniques.

As I look back on this journey, I have to conclude that it was by far the most important journey of my professional life. And I hope this book is of some help to teachers, at every educational level, who want to become partners with me on this journey.

ACKNOWLEDGMENTS

There are many people to whom I am deeply indebted for playing such pivotal roles in my becoming an interactive teacher. To Louis Raths, whose work began my journey, I owe a debt that can never be repaid. To my mentor, "Chris" Christensen, whose teaching and writing led me on the path to case method teaching, and who was a key figure in my life and work. For me, he is a giant in education and it is my great pride to acknowledge him and his work. To my buddy "down south," Larry Cuban, whose encouragement and support informed my best thinking. To the teachers who worked with me on the case method teaching project – Laura Bickerton, Richie Chambers, George Dart, Steve Fukui, Joe Gluska, Brenda McNeill, and Paul Odermatt – who taught me how perseverance and dedication to professional values and to the education of students was worth the effort. To my colleagues and friends, Maureen, Neil and Katie McAllister who are, to me, the best exemplars of how effective human interactions play such important roles in teaching and living. To my dearest Simon, the Wizard of Parksville, for all his help with every computer problem. And to my dear Jack, whose editorial wisdom I miss deeply, for him to know that flying solo is not for sissies. To all, my deep thanks and grateful appreciation.

1
INTERACTIVE TEACHING: THE WHAT, THE WHY, AND THE HOW

The stimulus for the class discussion was the case, "It's Up to You, Ms. Buscemi" (Wassermann, 1993) about a teacher who was torn between giving a Grade 12 boy the mark she believed he deserved, based on his classwork, homework assignments and test scores, and the principal's urging that she give the boy a better grade so that he would be able to enroll in post-secondary studies at a community college. The students had prepared by reading the case in advance, followed by working in small groups to address the study questions that accompanied the case. The case highlighted several critical issues, i.e., the actual academic performance of the boy based upon the teacher's ratings, the fact that he had to work part-time to help his low-income family, the competence of the teacher, the pressure from the principal, and the influence of the mark on his post-secondary school options. The class that read the case and prepared for the class discussion was a graduate education class that enrolled practicing teachers who were in a Masters of Education program.

She began her preparations for class discussion by first re-reading the case, highlighting what she considered to be the essential features, and then writing six "discussion questions" that would help her to focus the discussion on the important aspects of the case. She would keep this list of questions in front of her, to enable her to "stay on course" – i.e., to return to the important points if and when the discussion veered off course.

When she met the students that warm summer afternoon, they were seated in an informal arrangement of tablet armchairs scattered about in a large room. There was already a buzz in the atmosphere – she took that as a sign that the case was still "active" and fomenting. After greeting them, and asking them to place their name cards on the armchair, so that she would be able to call each one by his and her own name, she asked them first to give her a summary of the important

2 Interactive Teaching: The What, the Why, and the How

aspects of the case. Rather than use the "cold call" strategy of picking on a student who had not volunteered, she waited for hands to be raised – for some intrepid soul who would brave the first stage of the inquisition! For this she had to wait what seemed to be some long moments until a hand was raised.

"Yes, Ethan. Tell us how you would summarize the important features of this case."

As Ethan presented his views, she walked over to his chair, and stood close to him, focusing all of her attention on what he was saying. She listened carefully, making a mental note of his statements, and when he had concluded, "played them back" to him, in a more succinct way, capturing the essence of his views.

"Have I reflected your summary accurately?" she asked him.

He smiled and agreed that she had. The other students watched and understood the process.

"Would anyone like to add anything to Ethan's summary?" she asked, opening the discussion to call for further information that the students considered relevant. Several students raised their hands, feeling safer to respond now, and several additional points about the case were offered. These she also listened to carefully, making mental notes of the statements, and reflecting back the core ingredients of what had been said. With each student statement, she moved to that student's chair, and stood close by – giving her full attention to not only the statement but also to the student who was entering the discussion. Her first responses to the summary statements of the case were, by and large, reflective responses, holding up a mirror to what the student had said, and giving him or her a chance to further reflect on it – to see if she had accurately restated the key issues. In doing this, she demonstrated, through her behavior and through her reflective responses, that she had listened carefully, been respectful and free of judgment, and had given each student her full and complete attention, her behavior always indicating: "I am with you. I hear what you are saying and I am using that as working material to help you think further about the issues and about what you have said."

Only after the students had expended their views about the case summary did she raise the first question on her "crib sheet" of discussion questions.

"Tell me about the teacher. What can you say about her, and her teaching?"

Now the room was a flood of hands in the air, vying for "air time." Many in this group of practicing teachers had something to say about this teacher, Violet Buscemi, who had just taken her first job as a secondary math teacher in an inner-city school of a large city.

As was her style, she listened carefully to the statements being made, and without judgment or offering her own view, she reflected, at first by saying back the essential ideas, and moving on, asking students to examine assumptions, to identify value judgments, to think further about certain issues that warranted more examination. All of this she attempted to do in a non-threatening, non-inquisitorial style, so that the students would continue to feel comfortable offering their ideas. In raising the higher order questions, she was careful not to sound challenging, but rather as someone looking for further information, for clarification. Or as Christensen would call it, "teachers and students in a community of learners" (Christensen, 1995).

It was at this point that the discussion "took off" – with many students eager to offer ideas. She had made it safe for them to speak; and many of them had something they wanted to say. Each student statement was listened to carefully and respectfully, played back and sometimes, left hanging. Sometimes a further question was raised for clarification. Like a conductor of a Beethoven symphony, she knew when to cue in the timpani, and when to ask the string section for more crescendo. After much experience with discussion teaching, she had a keen hand and eye for when to shift gears to the next question, when to use reflective responses, when to raise clarifying questions, when to ask a "humdinger" – a question that would call for a deep, thoughtful, and wise comment.

The hour and a half of class time flew by – and by the end of the discussion, none of the issues in the case was resolved. This case, after all, was drawn from real classroom life, where there are seldom hard and fast answers, and where often, the "answers" depend on a particular point of view, a particular set of values, a particular orientation, and a view toward "what's important" in the teacher's and students' lives. At the end of discussion in cases such as these there is no closure but the niggling and jarring condition of "uncertainty" – so that the case is never finished in the students' minds – but like the pebble in a shoe, this will keep students thinking about it for a long time to come. It is this kind of interactive teaching that enables students to make meaning from experience (in this case, a case), allowing for greater insight and enriched understanding, leading to decision making that is based in data. In this process of meaning making, students grow in their intellectual power, in their ability to understand, and in their wisdom and maturity (Wiggins & McTighe, 2011). The teacher's skill and craft in conducting an interactive discussion is the key to that enriched intellectual experience.

Class Discussions and Class Discussions

Class discussions are not alien to teachers. They come in all sizes and shapes, and are seen at all levels of the educational hierarchy. Some of them are extraordinarily rich and productive – like the ones in evidence at the Harvard Business School (HBA), when a master teacher like "Chris" Christensen is "in the pit" conducting a case. Some of them involve a teacher-led discussion of a book, a film, a story, or a current event – where the teacher is the "point person," raising questions for students to answer, leading them to the core issues that the teacher wants examined. Some of them appear as discussions, but are actually stages for teachers to disseminate information, while students listen, take notes and, occasionally, raise a hand to ask a question (Wiggins & McTighe, 2011).

What may be more alien is the fact that some class discussions are so rich, so full of potential for student thinking and reflection, so challenging, that they have the capacity to leave students in a state of reflection long afterwards, trying to sort out discrepancies, making sense of complexities, working to resolve dissonance. And some discussions, drowned in teacher talk, lie like a beached whale, making the class seem a hundred years long, and leaving the mind dulled and opiated – as Professor Christensen liked to say, "instead of a teacher sitting on a log talking to a student, a teacher sitting on a student talking to a log."

What makes the difference? What does a teacher do to engage the minds of students in ways that open doors to discoveries, stimulate thinking and reflection, and enable and empower rational and logical reasoning? It is not obvious from the surface of a classroom observation – one has to know, to perceive, what it is we are looking for and looking at. We have to know more about what it takes for a teacher to dig into the minds of students and bring about more thoughtful, more insightful wisdom and understanding. We have to understand what Scott Turow learned in his student days at the Harvard Law School – that the teacher he had only lately learned to find of value was "some sort of jeweler of ideas, using questions like a goldsmith's hammer, working the concepts down to an incredible level of fineness and shine" (Turow, 1977). We have to allow that classroom discussions are not for giving students information – for that is more easily acquired through multitudes of high- and low-tech sources, and it is surely a waste of a teacher's time to do what other sources can do more effectively and more economically – but rather to elevate wisdom, to enable and empower critical thinking and logical reasoning, to help students make meaning of complex issues. This can be done more effectively through a process sometimes called "discussion teaching" and sometimes "interactive teaching."

> The lecture, the didactic form, will always be the primary method of teaching because it embodies the transfer of knowledge from expert to students. A good lecture is a work of art. But, the discussion method works best when teaching objectives shift from knowledge transference to student transformation – where qualities of mind (curiosity, judgment, and wisdom) become key. Or when academic goals demand the ability to apply concepts and knowledge to the solution of specific problems. (Christensen, 1995, p. 6)

At the very first, to do this, a teacher, no matter what educational level or subject area, must believe that this is the teacher's job. To wean oneself away from information dispensing to the higher and more challenging role of discussion leader is not for the faint-hearted. It is not easy to give up the role of master, and invert it, to become, with students, a "partner in learning." Having shifted gears, having risen to these challenges, the teacher is promised rewards that are not only observable, but much more satisfying. Students become more engaged; they are stimulated to think and to reason, and they are involved in what is going on in class. And the more the teacher "works" students' ideas, the more their thinking becomes more reasoned and more rational. This has been the case in virtually every "discussion teaching" class – from the Harvard Business School (Ewing, 1990) to Richie Chambers Grade 11 social studies class with the "Case of Injustice in Our Time" (Wassermann, 1992; Adam, 1992), to Bromley's work (1986) in psychology and related disciplines, to Eileen Hood's Grade 3 class where students were studying the "The Hockey Card" (see Appendix E). In fact, Bromley is quoted as saying: "The case for case-studies is made in terms of the pervasiveness of its employment in a range of human activities, from administration and anatomy, to politics and sociology, in terms of a basic methodology which underpins its use in these areas – the logic of scientific method."

But interactive teaching does not have to begin with a "case." It can begin with any other curriculum experience of significance – a story, a film, an article from a newspaper, an historical event, a Supreme Court decision, a TV program. The bases for interactive teaching are numerous and varied, and limited only by imagination and inventiveness. The Bill of Rights? Why not!

It is NOT the case, or other stimulus itself that does the work. It is the basis, the generator, of what follows, the interactive discussion that has the power to produce change in student thinking and behavior. Ewing (1990, pp. 9-10) in his insightful book about the "how and the what" of the Harvard Business School gives some evidence:

> You need only compare what comes in with what goes out. The incoming group was no more sophisticated than any other group of bright, energetic kids their own age might be. Their naiveté was colossal. Two years later, however, these same kids possessed a remarkable understanding, had an astonishing ability to put their arms about complex problems and analyze them, were able to make decisions with imperfect information with great skill, possessed penetrating insights into their own strengths, weaknesses, and aims in life.

Ewing also quotes John Russell, a senior professor at Boston University (Ewing, 1990, p. 10):

> Harvard does one thing better than any other school that I know of: it changes students. For nearly four decades I have seen this happen, over and over again. In the early first-year classes in September, I have seen students deal with cases in an amateurish way, missing the point, pontificating, applying glib rules of thumb, and making every mistake that a group of bright but wet behind the ears people might be expected to make. They would be so sure of themselves, it was frightening. Yet, in this class and study groups, subtle but profound changes would be occurring

in the quality of discussion and analysis. By spring, wondrous new abilities would be showing and during the second year, a true blossoming would take place.

What accounts for the difference? What teaching strategies are held as key to the improvements in students' behavior and ways of thinking?

At HBS, students are not taught in the way generally practiced by universities and training programs – that is, by lectures and reading. Rather, they learn by discussing cases that lack simple answers and making up their minds themselves in the presence of a master teacher. The theory behind that work is that students learn more realistically if presented with concrete problems from experience, and more thoroughly if they are forced to distill the lessons of those experiences themselves rather than be spoon fed the principles. (Ewing, p. 14)

Interactive Teaching – It's Not for Every Teacher

Having made a case for the importance of interactive teaching as a means of elevating students' higher order skills, and empowering them as independent thinkers, I must also add some caveats for those who might wish to consider this approach with their own classes. While I would, on the one hand, advocate it as an important methodology for the kinds of learning goals we say we want for all students, I would, on the other hand, recommend that teachers wishing to consider this approach reflect on their own personae, their own values about teaching and learning, their own psychological mind-sets before embarking on using interactive discussions.

So I offer some caveats for teachers to consider:

Interactive classrooms are places where the tension of uncertainty is elevated. There are no answers that are sought; rather discussions leave students often in a state of ambiguity – from which they are required to find their own resolutions. Does this kind of classroom seem exciting? Does it seem "wrong?" Does it raise hackles to think that students leave the room with unanswered questions, without closure (Richart, Church & Morrison, 2011)?

Teachers who are comfortable with the elevation of uncertainty, who have a higher tolerance for dissonance, who see productivity in not knowing and counter-productivity in absolute closure, are more likely to consider interactive teaching. Those who depend on the safety of absolute ground are likely to find interactive teaching discrepant with their core values.

Fred Fenster teaches economics to first-year students at a community college. He believes his job as a teacher is to give students information, that student learning involves receiving the correct information to build a strong knowledge base.

Fenster believes that only when students have the correct information will they be able to think about economic issues. Thinking occurs later, once the information is in place. He also believes that his particular skill as a lecturer makes for more effective information dispensing and knowledge building than is possible through written material. In his lectures, Fenster maintains tight control of the three important ingredients in a teaching/learning situation: time (when a task begins and how long it takes); operations (sequencing of lectures, monitoring students' mastery of concepts, monitoring mastery of procedures); and standards (monitoring control over student performance) (Berlak & Berlak, 1981). He is more than unlikely to choose interactive discussions; in fact, this methodology would be anathema to his educational goals.

A teacher's need for control is not a chosen value. It doesn't come from having made a conscious choice of how to behave. It rather comes from teachers' needs to feel "in charge," or to feel "on top of situations." Underlying this perception lies the thought that to "lose control" means losing one's effectiveness as a teacher. Teachers who are ruled by such needs are not likely to be persuaded to use interactive teaching in their classrooms. Control needs militate against the more open, more uncertain, more discordant interactive classroom.

On a final note, it should be remembered that interactive teaching is not a pedagogy that can be easily slipped into place in exchange for the more formal, lecture-type role. In order to be a successful discussion leader, one must work hard at developing the kind of skills required in learning to listen, to make sense of a student's statements, to select the appropriate responses, whether to reflect, to ask for examples, to interpret, to ask for criteria – in other words, to have an intimate awareness of how and when to challenge, and when to shift gears from one student to another. All of this assumes the mastery of skill that is the equivalent of the maestro conducting the symphony. The result, when it is successful, is the making of beautiful music. Underpinning all of that is the teacher's ability to learn to listen and watch him/herself in action – learning by doing – and reflecting on what is it that has been said and how. All of this one learns over time – with practice and reflection on practice. In other words, mastery as a discussion leader cannot be bought cheaply. It is earned through a long process of self-examination, and a non-defensive look at what one is doing in the act of teaching a group.

Important in this interactive process is the teacher's ability to step away from a teacher's most frequently heard responses of evaluating and judging. Teachers must learn not to say, "Good," or "That's right," or even, "That's an interesting idea"; they must step away from agreeing or disagreeing with a student's idea, and avoid leading the student to a particular line of thought or response or intimidating a student by being sarcastic or by dismissing an idea as not worth consideration. Any of these kinds of responses are killers – for they not only do damage to a student's self-esteem, but also are purveyors of the subtle message that the teacher is in charge, the fount of all wisdom, which the students must appreciate or be at risk.

Choosing Interactive Teaching

If teachers are considering the alternative of using interactive teaching in their subject areas, it is well for them to consider the caveats as well as the potential rewards of such choice. Interactive teaching feeds students' and teachers' sense of empowerment. Students gain in self-confidence and in heightened personal autonomy. They learn to become more responsible for what they say and how they say it and to reason more from the data and less from the seat of their pants. They learn to apply concepts and knowledge to the solution of specific problems. If these are a teacher's goals, then interactive teaching methods are unsurpassed in their ability to satisfy them.

Richie Chambers' Grade 11 social studies class was in session. They were discussing the "Case of Injustice in Our Time" – about the internment of Japanese Canadian and American citizens during World War II. The discussion was heated with points of view spanning the gamut from, "The Japanese got what they deserved; they bombed Pearl Harbor," to "What has that got to do with it?" to "How could a country like Canada take away the basic rights of its citizens?" As the discussion grew more heated, one Asian girl spoke up: "I have the terrible feeling that if this happened to my family today, none of you would stand up for us." A shudder went over the group that was palpable. The bell rang to signal the end of class, but the students lingered. Chambers looked at his students and then at the visitor, and said, "This is what social studies should be about" (Wassermann, 1992).

References

Adam, Maureen (1992). "The Responses of Eleventh Grade Students to Use of Case Method Instruction in Social Studies." Unpublished Master's Thesis. Vancouver, B.C.: Faculty of Education, Simon Fraser University.

Berlak, Ann, & Berlak, Harold (1981). *Dilemmas of Schooling*. London: Methuen.

Bromley, D. B. (1986). *The Case Method in Psychology and Related Disciplines*. Chichester: Wiley.

Christensen, C. Roland (1995). "A Community of Learners." *Harvard Gazette*, April 20, pp. 6–8.

Ewing, David (1990). *Inside the Harvard Business School*. New York: Times Books.

Ritchart, Ron, Church, Mark, & Morrison, Karin. (2011). *Making Thinking Visible. How to Promote Engagement, Understanding, and Independence for All Learners*. San Francisco: Jossey-Bass.

Turow, Scott (1977). *One L*. New York: Warner.

Wassermann, Selma (1992). "A Case for Social Studies." *Phi Delta Kappan*, 73(10), 793–801.

Wiggins, Grant, & McTighe, Jay. (2011). *Understanding By Design*. Alexandria, VA: Association for Supervision and Curriculum Development.

2
THE SHAPE OF TEACHING AND LEARNING IN THE INTERACTIVE CLASSROOM

What's the Big Idea?

Successful interactive teaching demands more than asking the right questions. Preparations for an interactive discussion begins with the teacher's identification of the big ideas: What are the important concepts that the students will address? What ideas will ground the discussion? On what fundamentals issues will the discussion be anchored? When the big ideas are clear, they give shape and meaning to the construction of the curriculum task in which students engage, and the questions and responses that will sustain the interactive dialogue (Wiggins & McTighe, 2011).

Identification of the big ideas upon which the curriculum task is created is the first step. The curriculum task may take a variety of forms and shapes. It may be a film, a case study, a law, a Supreme Court decision, a short story or chapter in a novel, a specific incident in the news, an editorial, an amendment to the Constitution, a scientific experiment, an advertisement, Executive Order 1066 – the options are vast. Of course, the task will necessarily reflect one or more aspects of the course curriculum – so the curriculum task selected is more likely to be based on course requirements.

It may be helpful to see how an elementary school teacher wrestled with the identification of the big ideas and the curriculum task he chose to enable students' examination of the big ideas through his interactive class discussion.

Jonah, an experienced Grade 6 teacher, wrestled with the concept of "teaching to the big ideas" for several weeks before he was able to understand the implications of this concept for his classroom work. He began by noting that "choosing one focus and carefully planning a sequence of activities that will teach one concept thoroughly is my goal."

As he struggled with his understanding of big ideas and compared that approach to how he had been organizing his curriculum activities, he noted, "I used to develop what I called 'themes.' We used to brainstorm a topic, let's say it was 'birds,' and then I'd bombard the children with countless activities all relating to the same theme. I realize now that most of those activities were busy work. They were fun. The kids enjoyed them (so did I!) but none of them really went anywhere. Just because they collected pictures of birds, made albums of bird photos, measured wing spans of big birds, made bird mobiles, and wrote poems about birds didn't mean that the students had a strong knowledge base that they could build on. Our 'higher level thinking skills' were not always higher, or involved any thinking. I feel that we were all caught up in the showmanship more than we were providing significant learning opportunities. Our rooms were dazzling, the atmosphere was fun, but it was shallow. That sounds quite harsh. I shouldn't throw out several years of effort, for indeed, kids did learn something. It's just that when I look at the units that I planned, I realize what was missing was the focus on the 'big ideas' – on concepts of substance and value that we could all build on. I tended to introduce too much, spend too little time on it, and give too much time teaching 'little skills' – those that could have been taught more effectively in another way. I'd spend a month on one theme and cover every aspect I could imagine until the topic was bled dry. I wonder now if many of those children still enjoy 'birds or 'water,' or even 'Ancient Egypt.' We were so busy flitting through related drama and art projects that we never had time to really stop and consider the deeper meanings – the beauty, the skill, the natural features of birds, and their importance in the natural environment (adapted from D. Dunn's personal journal, with permission).

In Jonah's notes, it is clear that while his earlier curriculum plans appeared well-constructed on the surface, he tended to devote time on activities that reflected a narrow range of ideas. Birds, whatever its potential for deeper inquiry, is not, in itself, a big idea. Nor is water. There are big ideas that may be generated out of the theme of birds, if a teacher wishes to do so. For example:

- Birds come in many different species, shapes, and colors.
- Birds range from small, and difficult to spot, to the large size of the bald eagle.
- Some birds are flightless; most fly and all have feathers.
- Many species undertake long migrations every year.
- Birds of prey are distinguished by their sharp bills and talons. They are fierce hunters.
- Shorebirds live along rivers, lakes and seashores and feed from the rich shallow waters of shores and coastlines.
- Humans have long depended upon waterfowl for food and feathers.
- The U. S. Fish and Wildlife Service reports that as many as 91 species of the nation's birds remain on the verge of extinction.

It's easy to see that when the big ideas are clear, they give direction to the kinds of curriculum tasks that allow for the ideas to be studied. Even more important, teaching to the big idea calls for pupils to study ideas of significance, of value, of power – ideas that have important larger meanings (Wiggins & McTighe, 2011). Teaching to the big ideas means that students' studies emphasize concept development, rather than details, or specific bytes of information. Conceptual understanding grows when learning tasks are provided in which students play around with big ideas (Feynman, 1985).

There are many examples of teachers missing out on the big idea in and around activities they have devised for their students. One example is the "famine" activity organized by a group of social studies teachers at the North Fork Senior Secondary School, to raise students' level of awareness of the tragic events taking place in Darfur, by giving them a taste of what it was like to experience a famine. The North Fork "famine" would last from Friday afternoon at 3:00 p.m. until Saturday at noon. Students would be allowed to have water, but no food. At the end of the session, the participating students would be honored at an assembly. It was a voluntary activity, but clearly many students thought of it as an adventure and were preparing to bring their sleeping bags, toothbrushes, cell phones, iPods, and CD players to entertain them through the long, hungry night. Darfur was much in the news at that time, and the social studies teachers, with the best of intentions, were looking for ways to bring the scope and depth of what was happening in that forsaken country "home" to their students.

To raise levels of awareness through experience is surely a good thing in teaching, but not every contrived experience teaches what is intended. So what was the big idea? And how did this curriculum activity deliver the important concepts that the teachers hoped to convey? Without having determined the big ideas to anchor the activity, the result was, at best, a sleepover for teens, who had plenty to entertain them during their "fast," and at worst, a trivialization of how people suffering from famine, with no recourse, starve and die (Wassermann, 2007).

Searching for the Meaning of Big Ideas

Some Ideas Are Very Broad in Their Scope

These very broad ideas are major generalizations. They may be topics rather than big ideas. They are often stated in more abstract ways. They tend to "cover the universe" in that they take in a vast territory. Because of their scope, they cannot be productively examined through short-term investigations and interactive teaching. They may need many investigations, and a variety of different curriculum experiences that occur over longer periods of time, in order to plumb the depths of the large concepts, so that students begin to comprehend the complexity and sophistication of these concepts.

Some very big ideas are:

- Natural resources are finite.
- Prejudice breeds hatred.
- Animals and plants adapt and change to survive in different environments.

- All sea life is interdependent.
- It is important for humans to have respect for the balance of nature.
- Culture is learned.

Some Ideas Are Big

Big ideas are often derived from key curriculum concepts. Students are able to grasp their meanings through focused investigative activities and interactive discussions. Productive examinations and interactive discussions enable students to comprehend, at deeper levels, the meanings of these big ideas.

Some examples of big ideas are:

- Effective social power arises out of the operation of inequalities present in group situations.
- Thinking is a way of learning.
- Pasteur's discovery of microbes led to the theory of germ disease.
- Various fuel sources produce energy.
- Sophisticated machines may reduce the need for human workers, leading to unemployment.
- Making a choice about a candidate for office is often burdened with "baggage" that is irrelevant to the candidate's competence.
- A set is a group or collection of things that are related.
- Stories are ideas that are told orally or written down.
- People tell stories to give information, to entertain and amuse, to make us think, to give us pleasure.
- In a democratic society, people have the right to vote to elect government officials to carry out the job of governing.
- What was a "scientific fact" yesterday may have been refuted by new scientific findings.
- Good listening skills help to build better human relationships.
- Germs can enter the body through the air we breathe, the food we eat, or the water we drink; through breaks in the skin; or through the bite of a carrier.
- The Nile River was essential to the rise of Ancient Egypt.
- The Bill of Rights is the name given to the first ten amendments to the U.S. Constitution.
- People see events through their own personal biases.
- There have been many periods in history characterized by rapidity of change leading to feelings of anxiety and unrest.

Some Ideas Are Very Limited in Scope (Small)

"Small" ideas focus on bits and pieces of information and are based primarily on facts rather than issues of significance. A value judgment or a biased point of view may be implied. Because they are limited in scope, they do not lend themselves to productive investigations or to rich interactive discussions.

Some examples of "small" ideas are:

- Magnets have two poles, one called North and one called South.
- Unlike poles attract; like poles repel.
- Ice is frozen water.
- Frogs hatch out of eggs.
- 1, 3, 5, 7 and 9 are odd numbers; 2, 4, 6 and 8 are even numbers.
- Blue and yellow when mixed will produce green.
- Columbus sailed the Atlantic Ocean in three ships, named the Pinta, the Nina, and the Santa Maria.
- The Pilgrims landed on Plymouth Rock in 1620.
- Canada has 10 provinces and the United States has 50 states.
- Pharaoh was the name given to the kings of Ancient Egypt.

Teachers who are searching the course curriculum for some big ideas to shape a curriculum task may be helped by the following questions:

- Is the idea too broad in scope? Is it a large, generalized concept that is too far-reaching to be studied meaningfully over several student investigations and interactive discussions?
- Is this big idea worthwhile? Does it have the capacity for a study of significance?
- Is it viable? Does it enable the creation of a curriculum task that will lend itself to inquiry of substance and value? (Is it worth spending time on?)
- Does it lead to an answer or to a set of answers, rather than an open discussion of key issues?

Big Ideas Lead to the Generation of a Curriculum Task or Investigation

An example of how a secondary school teacher, whose class was studying the Parliamentarian system of government, developed a curriculum task based on a big idea is offered as an example of the process:

An article appeared in a local newspaper entitled 'The Battle of the Breakfasts" which detailed how candidates at the Social Credit Leadership Convention were vying for the hearts and minds of the delegates by appealing to their stomachs.

Based upon this news article, and relevant to the upcoming elections in the province, the teacher considered the criteria for identifying some big ideas, i.e., is this a worthwhile idea for students to study? Does it have the capacity for a study of significance? Is it viable? Can it lead to an interactive discussion that would lend itself to an inquiry of substance and value?

From the news article, the following big ideas were identified:

- *The strength of a democracy is largely dependent on an informed electorate.*
- *The decision-making process is often burdened with excess baggage that is irrelevant to a candidate's qualifications.*
- *The "marketing" of candidates is intended to appeal to "non-essential" aspects that lie beyond a candidate's qualifications.*

Then, using the news article as a curriculum task, higher order questions were formulated that gave focus for students' small group discussion and examination of the big ideas.

- *How, in your view, do the voters at a leadership convention decide on the qualifications of a candidate?*
- *What kinds of information about candidates do you find persuasive?*
- *How do you assess the validity of what you see on TV and read in the newspapers about a candidate for office?*
- *Before making a choice about a candidate, what kind of information do you need?*
- *What kinds of assumptions do you see being made in making an electoral choice?*
- *How, in your view, should voters make choices? What are your ideas?* (Adapted from Wassermann, 1994, pp. 212-213)

These beginnings – i.e., the identification of the big ideas, the creation of the curriculum task and the formulation of the higher order questions for small group discussions – set the stage for the interactive discussion that follows.

Small Group Work

Not every teacher is an enthusiast of small group work; some, in fact, have even referred to it as "an exchange of ignorance." Yet, experience has taught us that small "study groups" that precede the whole group interactive discussion can benefit, in large measure, the outcomes of the whole group discussions.

One of the ways to contribute to the productivity of the study groups is to first ensure that all students have been given a chance to read and study the material in the curriculum task prior to small group work. It is no guarantee, but when the curriculum task is both interesting and has some meaning in the students' lives, they will more than likely come to class prepared to engage in more meaningful small group discussions. This is the equivalent of a homework assignment; some students will come prepared and others may avoid such responsibility. However, once caught up in the heat of the small group work, the student who comes unprepared is more likely to feel left out and his or her omissions will be easily identified and chastised by co-group members. It rarely happens twice. The onus is on the group to assume responsibility for productive discussions and they more than often rise to the challenge.

Group leaders, no matter what age level, seem to surface naturally and these students have been seen to "take charge" of chairing the small group sessions, keeping it on track, admonishing those who are unprepared, addressing unwarranted assumptions, and pointing out inadequacies in thinking. These productive sessions may not happen at the first sitting of study groups, but they are likely to emerge as groups gain power and strength in their reasoning abilities. There is something fine in watching students grow in their intellectual power to investigate issues and the big ideas. For teachers who observe these groups from an arm's length distance, the scene is more than satisfying.

Higher order questions focus the discussions in the study groups – and these are provided, in advance of the group work, along with the curriculum task. Higher order questions call for observations to be made, hypotheses to be suggested, assumptions to be examined, and comparisons to be made. They never seek a specific answer, but rather lead to open investigations about the issues (McTighe & Wiggins, 2013).

Small group work rarely ends with closure. In fact, this small group work is more likely to give rise to a variety of points of view about the issues. This is grist for the mill for what follows: the whole class interactive dialogue, in which the teacher will attempt to iron out discrepancies, put unwarranted assumptions under a rigorous eye, and open inquiry into the need for further information and deeper understanding of the issues under examination. Here again, the end of effort is not closure, but rather a learning to live with the uncertainties – so that students come to a richer understanding of the complexities and ambiguities of the big ideas. Tolerance for ambiguity is elevated as is increased ability to live with uncertainty. These are no small accomplishments (Watt & Colyer, 2011).

Follow-up Studies

If a curriculum task and the study group sessions drive the need to know, the whole class interactive dialogue heightens that need. How could this have happened? Students want more data! Because answers have not been given, because ambiguities have been elevated, tension is increased. The need to know grows more urgent. Motivation is high to read more, to find out. This is an important avenue for knowledge building. Information about the issues is not dispensed by some orderly schedule, but comes as a result of greater student need. This opens the door for the acquisition of relevant information – to expanding and extending the knowledge base.

Some curriculum tasks will already come with a healthy list of follow-up options. In some instances, teachers will draw on their own file of references: textbooks, articles from newspapers and magazines, tables and charts with primary data, research reports and projects, editorials and other commentaries, and other written information. Novels are another source of gathering perspectives on issues and are powerful resources. Films, both commercial and documentary, are a vital source of information and offer fresh perspectives. The use of Internet search engines to gather data should be examined and evaluated for accuracy. Follow-up activities may be carried out by individual students or in groups – however, most students enjoy working in teams, not only for the interplay of ideas and the use of various talents and strengths of different members, but as first-grader Eli liked to remind us: "It's eezeir when you have a buddy." Whatever follow-up activities are used, their value is enhanced by further interactive discussions, in which related issues get extended examination and new perspectives are introduced. Through this process, students' thoughtful, critical examination of the significant issues continually evolves.

How Long, Oh, How Long?

Teachers who are always in a race with the clock to get done all that needs to be done in a semester or term or school year will want to know: How long does this process of teaching and learning in the interactive classroom take – i.e., from the assignment of the curriculum task, to the study groups, to the interactive discussions and the follow-up? The answer to that is, like most answers in classroom teaching: it depends. Because above all, this is a matter of the teacher's judgment about the time students need for processing data. How much time should the issues be given? Some curriculum tasks take more time; some issues are more pressing and perhaps more current and relevant. Some may be given shorter shrift. There are no rules set in stone about the time cycle for teaching and learning in the interactive classroom. The teacher is always the best judge of how much time is allotted to the curriculum task, to the group work, to the interactive discussion and to the follow-up – keeping in mind that there is never enough time to do justice to all the issues, never enough time to discuss all the materials, and never enough time to teach everything. Time is always the good teacher's enemy, and each teacher learns, in his and her own ways, to resolve the ever-present conflicts between time available and "what's important."

References

Feynman, Richard (1985). *Surely You're Joking, Mr. Feynman*. New York: Norton.
McTighe, Jay, & Wiggins, Grant. (2013). *Essential Questions: Opening Doors to Student Understanding*. Alexandria, VA: Association for Supervision and Curriculum Development.
Wassermann, Selma (1994). *Introduction to Case Method Teaching: A Guide to the Galaxy*. New York: Teachers College Press.
Wassermann, Selma (2007). "Let's Have a Famine." *Phi Delta Kappan*, 89(4), 290–297.
Watt, Jennifer, & Colyer, Jill (2011). *IQ: A Practical Guide to Inquiry-Based Learning*. New York: Oxford University Press.
Wiggins, Grant, & McTighe, Jay (2011). *Understanding by Design*. Alexandria, VA: Association for Supervision and Curriculum Development.

3
PREPARING FOR INTERACTIVE TEACHING

Make no mistake. Interactive teaching is not for every teacher. And I would be disingenuous to pretend that it was any kind of panacea for lifting education from its bad reputation, including the exhaustive list of problems that plague teachers and students, or to claim it has the ability to address and remediate all of the failings cited in research and in the press. But I will say, with some confidence, based on data and experience, that interactive classroom discussions, thoughtfully and skillfully carried out, have the great capacity for transforming students from lesson learners into thoughtful, considerate, productive citizens (Barnes, Christensen & Hansen, 1994; McTighe & Seif, 2003). Teachers who have embarked on a program of interactive teaching have almost immediately seen positive results in their classrooms (Wassermann, 1992). The classroom ethos of interactive teaching is the focus of this chapter.

Tolerating Dissonance

"I don't have to know an answer. I don't feel frightened by not knowing things, by being lost in a mysterious universe without any purpose, which is the way it really is as far as I can tell. It doesn't frighten me" (Gleick, 1993).

The need for certainty, for the security that closure brings, seems to be a built-in part of our human makeup. When we've wrestled with dissonance, and have finally brought a situation to a conclusion, we feel a palpable sigh of relief, a sort of psychological "whew." There is no doubt about it – answers bring an end to uncertainty and therefore make us feel safe. Teachers may also experience a sense of accomplishment when our students can tell us that Ottawa is the capital of Canada and that Paul Revere designed the state seal of Massachusetts. Even experienced teachers who operate with a higher tolerance for ambiguity often wish for the relief that an answer can bring. Such a need for closure is especially true for beginning teachers who suffer from insecurities associated with their lack of experience and for whom "answers" provide the illusion that there are "fixes" to the profound and complex problems of teaching (Wassermann, 2001). Perhaps that is why so many of us look to our mentors, to workshops, to professional development days, and to the literature to tell us what is right. But in the end, as most teachers know, we are usually left to figure things out for ourselves – which requires both the stick-with-it capacity, the confidence in our ability to find a way, and the intellectual skills that enable that kind of problem solving.

This, of course, is the domain in which effective interactive teaching occurs – the uncharted territory where nettlesome problems are put under thoughtful scrutiny and where several possible courses of action appear reasonable. For those teachers taking their first steps into the territory of interactive teaching, where the quality of the inquiry is more important than arriving at answers, the prospect may be daunting. For teachers who are comfortable in such territory, the experience can be illuminating (Wassermann, 2009, pp. 22–23).

The teacher's ability to tolerate dissonance is a critical element of effective interactive discussions. To be able to do this skillfully is directly connected to the teacher's comfort with lack of closure. This requires, at the outset, a teacher's belief that this more open-ended kind of discussion is of benefit to students. It may be comforting to remember that it is "correct" answers that bring closure to all mental activity, that to know an answer does not an educated person make, and that knowledge alone is far from a guarantee that a person will behave intelligently, wisely, or competently. There is now a small library of articles, books, and essays that identify the attributes students need to develop for later life success, and none of them lists "knowing the right answers" as one (Costa & Kallick, 2008). A group of secondary school teachers identified what they hoped to see in their graduates. While these are, arguably, not the only behavioral goals teachers want for their students, it is interesting to note that no item on the list refers to the acquisition of factual information.

- Is able to understand big ideas
- Shows tolerance for the ideas and opinions of others
- Shows tolerance for discrepant data
- Is open-minded
- Is original, inventive, creative in work
- Has a high tolerance for uncertainty, ambiguity
- Is cautious in drawing conclusions; conclusions are based in data
- Is able to function on his/her own initiative
- Embraces thinking as a means of solving problems
- Is open and non-defensive in self-evaluation
- Is able to gather and organize data intelligently

- Is able to give examples in support of ideas
- Is able to generate hypotheses that are reasonable and are appropriate means of addressing problems
- Is able to make intelligent interpretations of data
- Is able to differentiate between opinion and fact; between assumption and fact
- Is able to make evaluative judgments that are rooted in appropriate criteria
- Is able to make thoughtful, intelligent choices with respect to problems, ethical issues and moral dilemmas (Adam, et al., 1991)

Interactive discussions in which the teacher can respond with "Tell me more" or "I'm wondering how you figured that out?" or "Perhaps you have some data to support your idea" are all invitations for students to examine further. They insist on clarity of thinking, upon reflection about a position, upon examples and data to support an idea. The discussion builds understanding at deeper levels of conceptualization and eventually leads to potential courses of action or more data gathering. It would be fair to say that teachers who engage students in such discussion teaching are building habits of intelligent thinking (Costa & Kallick, 2008).

Teachers who are making their first forays into interactive teaching may find the dissonance, at first, somewhat disconcerting. Yet, after time, many teachers find that relinquishing the need for closure that answers bring can be quite exciting.

Maintaining and Relinquishing Control

No teacher with a clear sense of what is important for the health, welfare, and education of students ever gives up total control over classroom functions. Not only would this be foolish; it would be dangerous. The teacher is always the adult in charge and the extent to which the teacher maintains and relinquishes control is decided by the teacher. It must also be said that the more control, in the form of decision-making capabilities, may be given to the students, the more students may learn to exercise their own controls responsibly. In this way, students are gradually empowered (Stefanou, Perencevich, DiCintio & Turner, 2004).

In an interactive discussion, teacher and students share control; they are partners in the learning process. The teacher has control over the choice of the curriculum task and over the amount of time that is going to be allocated to the group work and to orchestrating the interactive discussion – making the standards and the interactive process clear, deciding who speaks, how long, which response and questions are to be raised, when to shift gears to raise the next issue. The teacher also manages or controls the classroom climate in which the students feel safe to express their ideas. All of these facets of control are within the teacher's domain.

The students, on the other hand, have control over their own responses; there is no pressure to "give the teacher the answer that the teacher expects." No response is judged or evaluated as right or wrong, good or bad. Student responses are invited and given the same amount of "air time" and respectful attention. When the teacher judges a student statement to be "out of the ballpark" with respect to the quality of the idea, a response may invite the student to examine assumptions that are being made, to support the idea with data, to ask for examples. In this way, students learn to articulate their ideas, to submit them to intellectual scrutiny, to "be heard" and respected.

In an interactive discussion, the teacher, like the maestro, maintains control of most of the action.

But it is the students who have control over their ideas. And this is where the teacher relinquishes his or her control and gives students free reign to offer their ideas without implicit or explicit judgment or penalty.

Knowing Your Own Style

There is an ethos in a classroom in which successful interactive teaching occurs that goes beyond the skills required by the discussion leader. This ethos comes from not only the teacher's beliefs in the importance of involving students in an interactive process that raises levels of intelligent discourse, and the teacher's commitment to the kinds of learning goals that are the result of good interactive discussions, but also from the teacher's beliefs and attitudes that form his or her modus operandi. This is seen in the teacher's willingness to relinquish control and comfort with uncertainty, and an absence of defensiveness in the presence of tough questions and critical feedback. While some of these behaviors are learned, some are rooted in who we are and in what we consider our most cherished educational goals for students.

Tradition puts teachers in an elevated position, if not that of physically standing on a platform, then certainly in the time-honored image of teacher–student relationships. The portrayal of teachers as disseminators of knowledge and of students as empty vessels has a long and venerable history and it is what is most represented in documents, photographs, films, and stories about classrooms. The idea that a teacher has something, anything at all to learn from students is anathema to what most traditionalists think of when they picture classroom instruction. The apocryphal story about a teacher who was moving around the room providing individual instruction to students, while the principal made his supervisory observation and told her, "I'll come back when you're teaching," comes to mind (Wassermann, 1993).

Yet, in a classroom where the teacher cultivates a climate for intelligent discourse, "teaching objectives shift from knowledge transference to student transformation – where qualities of mind (curiosity, judgment and wisdom) and qualities of person (character, cooperation and open mindedness) become key" (Christensen, 1995, p. 7). What such transformation requires of the teacher involves some risk, for it means stepping away from the role of expert, shedding the garb of the all-knowing sage, and treading cautiously into the role of co-inquirer with students. Rather than dishing out morsels of information, teachers are asking questions; rather than declaring truths, teachers are trying to obtain the total involvement of the students. It requires thinking about the student first, not the subject matter; "when you get that involvement and bring both mind and emotion into the classroom, that's heady stuff" (Christensen, 1995, p. 8).

This of course does not mean that teachers should not know, or need not to know the subject matter of what they are attempting to bring to discussion. The teacher who is not only a master of the content, but equally knowledgeable about each student, is a master of the how – the steering of the interactive discussion.

Such an inversion of the traditional teaching–learning paradigm is likely to mean a significant shift in style – perhaps an entirely different set of clothes. A significant part of that is shedding the mantle of defensiveness that has protected teachers throughout history from any critical question, any deviation from the norm, any suggestion that they are less than powerful in maintaining dominance over all aspects of classroom life. That kind of defensiveness is doom for the effective interactive teacher (more about "observing oneself in the interactive process" is discussed in Chapter 9).

Establishing the Contract

If interactive teaching is new for teachers, it may also be revolutionary for students, especially those who have become accustomed to being passive listeners, tuning in and out as the spirit moves them, and responding only when urged or called upon. The interactive classroom puts new demands on students – to be more active and more intellectually engaged, and as in other new experiences, it is more effective when students are prepared for what is expected of them. Orienting the students to this new and different approach while being specific about expectations may forestall problems down the pike.

Students should know that preparation in advance of class is required. If the curriculum task is an historical document, they are expected to have read and studied it in advance of the class session. If it is an article, a film, a Supreme Court ruling, a series of photographs, or whatever, the students have a requirement to prepare the material by studying it and working to understand its surface and deeper meanings. While some students may, at first, shirk this aspect of preparation, it will soon be clear to them that not only are they at a loss when they are called upon to make a contribution to the small group discussions, but others in the group may call them out as having failed to do their part in assisting the group to build understanding. These reprimands from peers are strong persuaders that advance preparation is necessary for the process to work successfully.

Students should also be aware that they are required to participate fully and thoughtfully in the small group discussions that precede the whole class interactive dialogue. In order to ensure that these small group discussions are fruitful, each student is responsible for playing his and her part as a listener and a thoughtful and responsible interpreter of what other students are saying. Furthermore, guidelines for small group discussions should be clear: students learn to listen to each other, and to respond respectfully to each other's ideas. Respect for each other's thoughts and ideas is *sine qua non* in these discussions, and in that way, students learn the important lessons of being open-minded, tolerant of discrepant ideas, and respectful of their classmates. Learning to listen, to wait for others to speak, to interpret intelligently what is being said, to frame one's ideas clearly and thoughtfully are all significant learning experiences that derive from small group discussions. Some teachers may doubt the students' role in such a non-directive setting. However, the experience of many teachers in this process tells a different story – one that suggests that students can and do learn quickly to be responsible and additive group members when they are trusted and given the opportunity to participate at these higher levels of autonomy.

What part does the teacher play in these small groups? When the groups are well on the road to functioning smoothly and productively, teachers may keep their distance from them – and perhaps more important, because students are wont to "play to the teacher" if they perceive the teacher is standing by and listening in, thus robbing their autonomy. On the other hand, when groups are just getting started, the teacher may wish to take a bird's-eye view – to listen at arm's length, and to step in when and if the need to do so is critical. In most cases, it's a better plan to avoid intervening, and let the groups work out differences on their own. This has been known to occur, even in the elementary grades. Groups may, at first, struggle – and, initially, even find the time spent unproductive; but like most skills, working productively in small groups is a learned skill and students will eventually, perhaps with some small assists along the way, master this process and attest to its value. A helpful strategy is to ask students to "reflect on action" – that is, to engage them in examining the group work process *post hoc* – not only to evaluate how well the group worked together, but also to elicit suggestions for means and ways of improvement for the next sessions. I remember too clearly being reprimanded by one sixth-grader after a particularly contentious group work session, in which he heatedly told me, "If you had told us what to do, we could have done it in half the time. Look at all the time we wasted." And how sweet it was to see, after many long trials, the groups not only functioning effectively, but owning their autonomy as their right.

Preparing for the whole class interactive discussion may also require some advance groundwork, as the expectations and the modus operandi may be very different from students' earlier classroom experiences. So setting the stage, and making expectations and the process clear, may offset later problems.

While each teacher's interactive style may differ, there are certain facets that are in evidence in all interactive discussions. Students should know that they will not be called upon; there are no "cold calls" – unless they volunteer their ideas. (At first, this may take some "wait" time – because students may be reluctant to offer ideas, having paid the price, in earlier experience, of being rebuked for a wrong answer.) They should know that each idea offered will be listened to respectfully and "used as working material" – that is, the teacher will use a selected group of responses and questions to help a student clarify his or her thinking and perhaps dig for deeper meanings. The students may also be told, in advance, that if and when a student "on the hot seat" does not wish to engage further, he or she has the "option" to let the teacher know. In other words, students have control over when they wish to respond, and how long they wish to engage in the process with the teacher in the interactive discussion. There are no penalties or rewards for students' responses.

Students may also be told that the interactive discussion is not a call for answers, but a request for thoughtful, intelligent thinking about the issues. No evaluations are given for student responses. All responses are treated as grist for the inquiry mill – and this is part and parcel of the process of interactive discussions.

Orienting students to the process need not be a long-term activity, but ensuring that expectations, procedures, and goals are clear will, at the very least, provide important information to the non-initiated. The following list of suggestions may be helpful:

- Introducing students to the methodology and describing the process – the study of the curriculum tasks, small group work, and whole class interactive discussion – and allowing students to raise questions about any of this may forestall problems of misunderstanding expectations and requirements.
- Telling students what you consider to be the benefits of this way of teaching may be a valuable lesson for them – since this methodology puts considerably more onus on them as learners. In fact, they should know that while this methodology raises new challenges for them – especially those who have been habituated to more traditional classroom practices – the rewards can be great in terms of building intelligent habits of mind.
- It is probably a good idea to be explicit about your expectations at the outset. Students should know that you expect them to be prepared; to have read and studied the curriculum task; to participate responsibly in small group work; and to volunteer their ideas in the interactive discussion. For without students' full participation in these stages of interactive teaching, the success of the pedagogy is imperiled. While all of this may not occur at the outset, thoughtful and deliberate evaluation of the process along the way is a helpful way of furthering students' learned skills in the process.
- Since marking and grading are often *the* primary movers and shakers in the educational process, students will want to know, at the outset, how the teacher is going to evaluate their work. That is why it is a good idea to make your plans known – i.e., what evaluative procedures will be used, what criteria are to be used in evaluation, and how grades will be determined. Consistency, fairness, and openness to students' concerns will go a long way in alleviating the stress around evaluation. However, whatever evaluation methods are used, they should be consistent with the ethos of interactive teaching. Otherwise, students

will learn that the behaviors necessary to pass the test (not those necessary for thoughtful, intelligent discussion of issues) are the ones that really count.
- Not every student will find it easy to be a productive member of an interactive discussion. Some will find it difficult to handle the freedoms that are integral to this kind of classroom, where students must assume more responsibilities for their participation and learning. Some may, understandably, wish to retreat, to return to the safety of a teacher-dominated discussion, where they are told what to do, and how. (We grow to love our chains?) A bit of empathy for the stresses that interactive teaching puts on students may go a long way in helping students to overcome the anxieties they may initially feel as they move along the pathway of becoming more independent thinkers.

Teachers who have watched students struggle with the demands of new programs — especially those that put greater burdens on students to behave more responsibly and more actively in the learning process — will be sympathetic to the necessity for good orientation for the students for each stage in the process, remembering that many skills are not learned in one sitting and that, for some students, it may take a bit of time to become more adept and more engaged in the process. For no matter how effective the orientation may be, and no matter how skillful the teacher in preparing, there is no magic kiss that turns frogs into princes.

As a final note to this chapter, it is recommended that at the end of each interactive discussion (after the students have prepared, participated in small group work, and engaged in the whole group dialogue), the teacher ask the students to reflect, in retrospect, on the whole of the process. What do they see as some benefits of their *a priori* studies of the curriculum task? What would they like to say about the small group discussions, primarily with respect to how they benefitted from this first examination of ideas about the task? What did they find of value in the whole group interactive process? What were some weak points of the process? What were some strengths? What should be considered for the next session to facilitate the process? For example:

- How did you see your work in the small group session as helpful to you in your thinking about the issues?
- How did you see the whole class discussion as helpful to you in your thinking about the issues?
- What were some important features of the small group session that were helpful to you in thinking more about the issues?
- How do the small group sessions and the whole class discussion help your communication skills?
- How does this process contribute to your respect for the ideas and opinions of others?
- What responsibilities do you see yourself having in this process? How do they benefit you as a learner?

- How does this process enable you as an independent thinker? Learner?
- What are some of your frustrations with this methodology?
- What ideas do you have for improving this work for the next class?

These are not the only questions that can be asked – but they provide examples for how teachers may raise awareness in students of how they benefitted from the process so that students and teacher may use their ideas as a way of ensuring that all may benefit from that reflection on the process in subsequent sessions.

References

Adam, Maureen, Chambers, Richard, Fukui, Steve, Gluska, Joe, & Wassermann, Selma (1991). *Evaluation Materials for the Graduation Program*. Victoria, BC: Ministry of Education.

Barnes, Louis B., Christensen, C. Roland, & Hansen, Abby J. 1994. *Teaching and the Case Method*. Boston: Harvard Business School.

Christensen, C. Roland (1995). "A Community of Learners." *Harvard Gazette*, April 20, pp. 6-8.

Costa, Arthur L., & Kallick, Bena (2008). *Learning and Leading with Habits of Mind: 16 Essential Characteristics for Success*. Alexandria, Virginia: Association for Supervision & Curriculum Development.

Gleick, James (1993). *Genius: The Life and Science of Richard Feynman*. New York: Vintage.

McTighe, Jay, & Seif, Elliot (2003). "A Summary of Underlying Theory and Research Base for Understanding by Design." Unpublished manuscript, available at your-space.wiki.usfca.edu.

Stefanou, Candice R., Perencevich, Kathleen C., DiCintio, Matthew, & Turner, Julianne C. (2004). "Supporting Autonomy in the Classroom: Ways Teachers Encourage Student Decision Making and Ownership." *Educational Psychologist*, 39(2), 97-110.

Wassermann, Selma (1992). "A Case for Social Studies." *Phi Delta Kappan*, 73(10), 793-801.

Wassermann, Selma (1993). "It's Up to You, Ms. Buscemi." In Wassermann, Selma, *Getting Down to Cases*. New York: Teachers College Press, pp. 156-161.

Wassermann, Selma (2001). "Shazam! You're a Teacher! Facing the Illusory Quest for Certainty in Classroom Practice." *Phi Delta Kappan*, 80(6), 464-468.

Wassermann, Selma (2009). *Teaching for Thinking Today*. NY: Teachers College Press.

4
SCENES FROM INTERACTIVE CLASSROOMS

Those of us who have been lucky enough to study a master teacher in the act of conducting an interactive discussion will have learned the "how to" in the most effective ways possible. It is through this kind of sustained observation that one begins to understand about the various and interwoven threads of an interactive dialogue, e.g., how to approach a student in the opening call for a response; how to listen and attend to a student's statement; how to process that statement and choose an appropriate response; how and when to raise a challenging question, or not; how and when to "end" the interactive dialogue with that student and move on to another; how to keep the important issues alive and under scrutiny – and all the small and large other factors that keep an interactive discussion on track and productive. It is not different from learning to play the violin. Listening to a maestro perform gives one the sense of what the music can sound like. The rest, as they say, is practice, practice, practice and learning to listen to oneself in the process.

Learning by observation, however, may not be possible as a starting point for most teachers – especially if interactive teaching is "foreign territory" in a school, a school district, or an academic department. If that is the case, turning to a descriptive text may be the next best option. Thus, to set the stage for a virtual observation of those basic interactive skills (listening, responding and questioning, of which each strategy is given its own chapter), it may be helpful to begin with an overview – some dialogues of interactive teaching – so that the process may be examined in virtual reality.

The Train

Centennial Secondary School lies in a suburban community to the east of a large Canadian city. Students come from well-kept, single-family homes; parents are professionals and/or of the middle and upper middle class. There is a healthy mixture of ethnic groups and students mingle easily with each other. The school has a reputation for academic performance, and serious-minded students from out of the school catchment area may apply to enroll. The hallways, between classes, show an informality and an ease of passage.

George Broadbent teaches Art History – an elective course for juniors and seniors that generally has a full enrollment. He is an artist himself, but his heart is in teaching. His mission, as he sees it, is to enrich the lives of his students by giving them entry into the world of fine art – from an historical as well as a contemporary perspective.

In preparation for today's discussion, the students have, in a previous session, viewed the film *The Train* – an "oldie" that stars Burt Lancaster and Paul Scofield. It is set in France, during World War II, and there is plenty of action for today's overly saturated with violence teens. Briefly, the film is about the French underground's initiative, near the end of the war, to save the great works of the Louvre and the Jeu de Paume from being stolen by the Germans and transported to Germany. Burt Lancaster plays a train engineer – one who has little or no understanding of why art is so important that lives must be put at risk to save the paintings. Scofield is the quintessential Nazi colonel – a connoisseur of fine art, who will stop at nothing to acquire the paintings for himself and see them transported to his country. The film is loosely based on true events, and documents the way the Nazis planned to loot priceless works of art from museums and private collections and have them shipped to Germany, no matter the cost in lives. The urgency of the mission is heightened by the news of the imminent liberation of Paris by the Allies. The French underground needs to delay the train only for a few days – without damaging the cargo.

The students have seen the film and met in their study groups, discussing the questions that George provided and that would prepare them for the whole class interactive discussion that would follow.

George prepared himself by re-viewing the film, and by preparing a set of questions to keep him on track in focusing the discussion on the big ideas. He had identified the big ideas as:

- The value of art masterpieces cannot be calculated in any real sense.
- The value of great art is determined by those who appreciate it.

The class is not new to interactive teaching and George opens the discussion by asking his first question:

> GEORGE: Who wants to take the initiative and summarize the key points of the film?
>
> There is the usual long wait for a volunteer. George smiles and waits it out.
>
> SHIRLEY: I'll try, Mr. Broadbent. The Nazis stole some famous paintings from the museum in Paris and want to ship them back to Germany. But the

French Resistance wants to keep them in France. The allies and their armies are getting close – and they have to hold the paintings until the armies can rescue them.

GEORGE: Thanks for taking the first shot, Shirley. I appreciate it. Let me see if I can paraphrase what you have told us. The paintings are famous and valuable. The Nazis want to remove them and ship them to Germany. But the Resistance group says they need to hold out, and hold onto the paintings until the Allied forces liberate the country. Have I represented what you have said accurately?

SHIRLEY: Yes, Mr. Broadbent. But there's one thing I want to add. The Nazis have put the paintings on a train to ship them home. So the French need to do everything they can to keep the train from going to Germany.

GEORGE: The train is the important element in this story. The pictures are on the train and the French Resistance must prevent the train from getting through to Germany.

SHIRLEY: Yes, that's right.

GEORGE: Thanks, Shirley. Does anyone want to add anything to Shirley's summary?

MALIK: Yeh. The guy that is given the job to keep the train and save the paintings does not really appreciate art, or the value of the paintings. But the guy, the Nazi, who wants the paintings, does!

GEORGE: One important feature of the film is the tension between the two men. The one who has been given the job of saving the paintings and the train has no appreciation of the value of the masterpieces. But the Nazi, Colonel Waldheim, has a great appreciation of the value of the paintings.

MALIK: Yeh. And I want to say this too. It kinda puts the film in a strange frame – because the guy who risks lives to save the paintings doesn't know or appreciate their value. He doesn't understand the reason for having to risk lives to do this job.

GEORGE: The Nazi – who is looting the paintings – has a great appreciation of the art; but the Frenchman, Labiche, is doing the job without any appreciation of the worth of the paintings.

MALIK: Yeh. It puts a twist on the film that makes for more tension, I think.

GEORGE: Thanks Malik, for adding that to our understanding of the issues in the film. I want to ask you about the main characters – Labiche and von Waldheim. What observations have you made about them?

KARIM: I want to talk about Labiche, as he is an interesting character to me. He is a good trainman, or do you say, engineer? He knows trains and he knows the people who run the trains. That is a big help to him in what he is trying to do. He doesn't seem to be afraid for his own life – but he keeps wondering if all those people have to die because of a few paintings. He is not an art appreciator!

GEORGE: You find it curious that while he, Labiche, has taken this job to save the train and the paintings, he, himself, is not an art appreciator. He is a good engineer, but hardly a person who appreciates fine art.

KARIM: Yeh, I think that makes for the tension in the film. He is constantly searching himself to see if the lives lost are worth the value of the paintings.

GEORGE: Labiche is a critical character – because it is within him that the tension between the value of lives and the value of the paintings rests.

KARIM: Yeh, that's right. Are the lives lost worth the value of the paintings?

GEORGE: You see that as a central issue in the film. Thanks, Karim. How about the Nazi colonel? What would you like to say about him?

EWEN: He's tough and arrogant. He thinks he should have the paintings because only he knows the value of them and only he can truly appreciate them.

GEORGE: Am I seeing something behind your words, Ewen – that you hold some animosity towards the colonel? For who he is and for what he stands for?

EWEN: Yeh! Just because you appreciate something more than others, that doesn't mean you are entitled to take them for yourself. That's stealing.

GEORGE: Colonel von Waldheim has no right to claim the paintings. They don't belong to him. Love of art does not entitle you to steal what is not yours.

EWEN: Well, that's what the Nazis did anyway. They took from all the occupied countries, and made off with the loot to enrich themselves. They were no better than thieves.

GEORGE: So the paintings did not actually belong to the Nazis. And Colonel von Waldheim had no rights to them.

EWEN: Yeh.

GEORGE: Thanks, Ewen. I want to shift gears now and ask about where you stand with respect to this whole operation of saving the paintings. Many lives were lost – and this was the price they had to pay to save the pictures. What do you think? Was it worth it?

JEANNE: Well, Mr. Broadbent, that's a hard question. Because if you look at it from a distance – well, who were these people who lost their lives? Do they matter to us? But if your father or your brother or your mother had to pay with his life, then it would be a different story.

GEORGE: You think, Jeanne, that it matters who the people were – if you cared for them, you would not want them to lose their lives over some paintings. But if they were strangers, it wouldn't matter to you.

JEANNE: Oh – no, that's not what I meant. Lives are important – no matter whose lives. But the lives of people you care about are more important.

GEORGE: All lives are important – no matter. But some lives are more important than others?

JEANNE: Yeh. (Says hesitatingly)

GEORGE: So we come to the heart of the issue – the value of the paintings. What value has been put on them? What do you think about that?

SAM: Obviously, the French Resistance put a great value on the paintings. They wanted to save the paintings at any cost. And lots of lives were lost.

GEORGE: The French put a very high value on the art – and were willing to risk people's lives to keep the art from being shipped to Germany.

SAM: Yes. And I'm not sure where I stand on that. If the worth of the art is worth more than the lives of people.

GEORGE: You're undecided. You don't know if you would put a higher value on the paintings than on the lives of people.

SAM: Yeh, that's what troubles me. I don't know the answer. Maybe that's because I don't value the art myself. Perhaps if I felt about the art the way the German colonel felt, I would be on the side of the paintings.

GEORGE: So you really have to love the paintings so much, that you would be prepared to make such huge sacrifice in lives for them.

SAM: I guess so.

GEORGE: Can you love something so much that you would be willing to sacrifice lives? That seems to be the crux of the matter here. So I'll leave that for you all to think about – and suggest some readings to follow up. But also, I'm recommending a trip to the museum downtown to see the Picasso exhibit and we'll talk again tomorrow. Thank you all for sharing your ideas.

George Broadbent started the discussion with the opening question, asking for the highlights, in summary form, of the film – keeping in mind that he will eventually steer the discussion, through responses and questions to the examination of the big ideas. He waits for a volunteer – choosing not to use the "cold call" – because he believes that to be less intimidating and he prefers a softer approach. His first few responses to students are largely in the paraphrasing domain – and only when the discussion "takes off" does he move to some higher order questions. It is apparent, even from reading the transcript, that he listens carefully to each student, responds respectfully to each statement, values what is being said, and uses the student's statements to bring about their further reflection on their ideas. At the very end, he leaves the ideas open – in the expectation that students will continue to think and discuss the various aspects of the issues. He also has, at the ready, suggestions for further study that focus on art and values. There is much more that can be mined in these studies – and George will be deciding how far and to which aspects of the issues he wants to take the discussions in the next classes.

Germs Make Me Sick!

Laura Silverstone teaches Biology 12 at a large urban school in one of the major cities of the United States. The school is in a residential area, and enrolls a large population of ESL students, mostly Asian. The parents are working class, and their interest in the education of their children is palpable, as they see school and learning as the primary way to succeed in their new country. Laura's class is in the academic stream, and there are few, if any, "behavioral" or discipline problems. Students are generally well prepared, having done their homework faithfully and turned their assignments in on time.

The class has been studying germ theory, disease, and epidemiology – the study and analysis of the patterns, causes, and effects of health and disease conditions, with a view toward how these studies affect policy decisions, risk factors for disease, and preventive health care.

In preparation for the discussion the class has read the case, "An Incident in Boston" (Ochoa, 1999)[1], which introduces students to ideas about influenza viruses, how they are transmitted, the dangers involved, and methods of protection. They have also met with their study groups to discuss the questions the teacher has prepared in advance of the interactive discussion.

The case rests on the following big ideas:

- Influenza is a respiratory disease caused by an influenza virus.
- Swine flu is one type of influenza virus.
- Influenza virus is unique among respiratory viruses in its ability to undergo continual antigenic change.
- Influenza cannot be treated by antibiotics.

> LAURA: You've all read the case, "An Incident in Boston" (Ochoa, 1999) and you've had some chances to discuss the case and respond to the study questions in your study groups. So now I want to ask you a few questions about the data you've gathered, and what kinds of understandings you've arrived at in the course of your reading and discussions. Let me begin by asking what you have learned about the Spanish flu from your reading of the case?
>
> KIM: I know that it was a huge epidemic and that it happened right after World War I and that was important because they didn't have the facilities at that time to deal with it.
>
> LAURA: Tell me what you mean by "facilities," Kim.
>
> KIM: I mean they didn't have the vaccine and they didn't have the equipment to identify the virus that was causing the flu – like the right kind of microscope.

LAURA: A flu vaccine and a more powerful microscope might have been helpful since the virus was so small. Thanks, Kim. Does anyone want to add to what Kim has begun telling us? Yes, Mei?

MEI: Wait a sec, let's see. I want to refer to my notes about the case. Okay. I know that the flu killed millions of people all over the world – and that's why they called it a pandemic – because it was a worldwide disease. I think they said that the flu killed more people than were killed in the war.

LAURA: The number of deaths were staggering. They had no means of combatting the disease.

MEI: Yeh. And what's more, the movement of people – that is, the soldiers who were contaminated were moved out to other locations and this spread the disease everywhere. And they didn't have a good idea of how it was being spread. And that's what the case said – that the war was the flu's best friend.

LAURA: The soldiers who were infected were shipped out and they were the carriers of contamination. The people in charge didn't know, at the time, how the disease was being spread. Thanks, Mei. Anyone else want to add anything more about what you read about the Spanish flu?

AL: I was puzzled about the way the medical researchers went about trying to find out what to do. I thought the process was much more simple and I was surprised to learn how much in the dark they were when they started and they really didn't know what to do!

LAURA: The process of how the medical scientists went about determining what they could do was a surprise to you. You thought that carrying out medical research was a good deal more straightforward. You were surprised that even these learned scientists had no clear idea about how to proceed.

AL: Yeh, they were just a bunch of guys sitting around a table trying to figure out the best strategies and they didn't even agree!

LAURA: When even these high-level scientists don't agree on what to do, it's hard to find the right procedures. How are we to know?

AL: Yeh. It gave me a better idea of how scientists deal with unknown diseases. And I hadn't been prepared for the way some of them let their egos rule their decisions.

LAURA: That surprised you too – that doctors and research scientists don't agree and some of them have egos on the line that steer the way they think and choose. What, if anything, does that do to undermine your trust in them?

AL: Ouch! You need to depend on your doctors for the right prescription, for the right diagnosis. And maybe you should be more cautious and get second opinions in serious cases.

LAURA: That gave you much to think about, Al. Many thanks for sharing your ideas. Now, how about how the Spanish flu pandemic compares with the current concerns about the Zika virus. What data have you gathered about that?

Laura proceeds in this interactive rhythm, moving from data gathering questions, to questions calling for hypotheses, and finally to questions about way is in which we, today, may take precautions against infection from a virus.

At the close of the interactive dialogue, Laura gives students an assignment to do some follow-up reading about the influenza virus and distributes the article, "What We Now Know About the Influenza Virus," by Carolyn Bridges, M.D., and then reminds them that a self-evaluation sheet will be distributed at the close of the unit so that they may make their own determinations of the extent and quality of what they have learned about the influenza virus. Laura also plans to schedule the filming of *The Boys in the Band* about the early days of the AIDS virus and how scientists and the public responded to the spread of that disease.

There are, of course, many different ways of responding to students' statement, including the kind of response chosen, as well as the way the response is worded; whether to question or to paraphrase; whether to ask for an example, or to ask for more information; or whether to interpret, or to ask that assumptions be examined. The bottom line is that many responses are viable – provided they are respectful, enable the student to think about the statement, and lead to the further examination of the big ideas. To keep the dialogue open, responses that give closure or make a value judgment should be avoided.

The Hockey Card

The two examples above demonstrate interactive discussions at the secondary school level. But what about elementary school? Eileen Hood wrote the case of "The Hockey Card,"[2] based on an incident that occurred in her Grade 3 classroom. Eileen taught in an elementary school, in a suburban school district outside of a major city. The students came from single-family homes, in a residential area. They were a mixed group – Caucasian, Asian, and a few First Nations students who came from a nearby reservation. The classroom incident occurred when one of the boys brought a very precious hockey card that was signed, personally, by a famous and highly valued ice hockey player. The boy's friend asked him if he would allow him to take the card to his class to show his own classmates, and the boy agreed. Having done that, for whatever reason, the card went missing. The question of who was responsible was one issue. Additionally, the teacher wanted to center the interactive discussion on the appropriateness of bringing valuable items to school.

It should be noted that the case of "The Hockey Card" was written after this situation occurred in Eileen's class. So the interactive discussion came about as a result of the loss of the card. No prior reading or small group discussion paved the way for the whole class discussion. Eileen did, however, have a clear idea of the big ideas for the discussion:

- When people decide to lend their belongings to others, the lender and the borrower may have obligations and responsibilities that are implied in the transaction.
- Sometimes, you have to deny your friend's request in order to protect your valuable property.
- Being generous with your own things may backfire and cause you a loss that you had not anticipated.
- It may not be a good idea to bring valuable items to school.

> EILEEN: We had some trouble in our class. David brought his hockey card to school – the card that was signed by Wayne Gretzky. And Billy, from the Grade 3 class down the hall, asked David to let him take the hockey card to show to his class. David gave Billy his card, with the expectation that Billy would return it to him at lunchtime. But somehow, the card went missing and Billy doesn't know what happened to it. Before we get into the question of what David SHOULD do now, what can you tell me about David and Billy?
>
> STEVE: I think that David should not have loaned Billy the card. Because if you have something valuable, you don't want to take a chance of losing it.
>
> EILEEN: Yes, thank you Steve. I'm wondering what you can say about David and about Billy first, before we get to what David should have done. What can you tell me about David?
>
> NOREEN: I think David was being very nice to Billy. But he shouldn't have let him take the card.
>
> EILEEN: David was a good friend to Billy. He was kind enough to lend his card.
>
> NOREEN: Yes. And it was a mistake.
>
> EILEEN: Sometimes, we do things for a friend that cause problems for us.
>
> NOREEN: Yeh. You shouldn't take a chance to give something to a friend, if it is too valuable.
>
> EILEEN: Even if it is a very good friend and you want to help him out.
>
> NOREEN: Yeh. But sometimes, you have to give it.
>
> EILEEN: Sometimes, you want to be generous with your things. But you can't know what is going to happen when you lend something you care about. David, do you want to tell us what you think?
>
> DAVID: I thought he would take care of it. I really didn't want to lend it to him. I was worried when I gave it to him. But he said he would take care of it. My dad is going to kill me.

EILEEN: You really didn't want to give your card to your friend. But he put some pressure on you to lend it to him. In spite of how you felt, you gave it to him anyway. And now, you are going to be in trouble with your dad.

JASON: I want to talk about Billy. He should have looked after the card. He's responsible. He should pay David or get him another card.

EILEEN: You think that it's Billy's fault. He didn't look after the card. He should have taken care that the card was safe. And he didn't do that. He's responsible for fixing the situation. He should pay David or get another signed card.

JASON: Yeh. I'd be so mad at Billy.

EILEEN: David should be angry at Billy. Billy was irresponsible. He needs to make amends. But there's another issue that I want to ask about. What about bringing valuable items to school? What do you think about that?

Eileen opens the discussion with a question that asks about the two boys, and Steve jumps in to suggest what David *should* do. But Eileen wants to address the question of the "players" first, so she acknowledges what Steve has said, and gently shifts the discussion to her *a priori* question. She has to be particularly sensitive in this discussion to ensure that David's feelings are respected and that he has a chance to voice his own position as well as listen to what others have said. There will be much more discussion before Eileen moves to the final question of action – what is to be done. In all of this, she hopes that ideas will be forthcoming about lending valuable items to friends as well as the question of bringing valuable items to school, and that students will be supportive and not critical of David.

Not every discussion is based on a case, or a film, or a pre-arranged activity that comes from the curriculum of the course. Some incidents, like the loss of the hockey card, may come from an unanticipated class event – and from that, an interactive discussion may proceed. In other words, many class experiences, including those that are curriculum-based, are grist for the interactive mill. Whichever the situation, the principles of an interactive discussion are maintained: listening, choosing the appropriate response, and raising higher order questions that dig deeply into the big ideas. Underlying all is the teacher's overt and covert show of respect for the students and for what they have to say.

The Grade 2 class had come to the university to participate in a group discussion, demonstrating interactive teaching to a class of pre-service teachers. The children were examining a photo of a fish skeleton, and were making some observations about skeletal structures, all of which were listened to by the teacher, and then "replayed" with paraphrases, as well as some higher order questions.

Shaun wanted to add his ideas about the fins of the fish and said:

SHAUN: There are the fins. But the fish didn't always have fins, you know. They had feet. And then the feet turned into fins.

The teacher, non-plussed, said, "So at one time, the fish had fins and they turned into feet?"

> SHAUN: No, the feet turned into fins!
>
> TEACHER: (Trying not to laugh, looked down at her feet.) Ah, Shaun, do you think that will happen to me?
>
> SHAUN: *Serious.* No, because it takes a hundred years.

You can never be fully prepared for what is coming out of the mouths of your students – but it is, at the very least, precious to be given the chance to hear what they think.

Copies of videos of Interactive Teaching are available from the publisher.

Notes

1. The Spanish Flu unit may be obtained from the College Board online at: www.collegeboard.org.
2. A copy of the case "The Hockey Card" may be found in Appendix E. It is included with permission from the author.

References

Ochoa, George (1999). "An Incident in Boston," in *The Spanish Flu and Its Legacy*. New York: The College Board.

5
BASIC INTERACTIVE SKILLS: LISTENING, ATTENDING, APPREHENDING, MAKING MEANING

On the surface, it seems a "no-brainer" to suggest that teachers listen and attend to what students are saying. However, in the pressure-cooker atmosphere of a classroom with its many demands on teachers and many hands vying for that teacher's attention, it is far from easy to listen, attend, and apprehend in an effort to pay full attention to what a student is saying – to make meaning of the statement and its implications, of the emotionality that may lie behind it, of the hidden agendas – and to use what is apprehended to construct an appropriate response. Listening is more than just hearing the words. It includes observing all behavioral cues as the words are being spoken; hearing nuance and voice inflection; observing particular words chosen to express certain ideas; and noticing where the statement is given emphasis. When all of that occurs, the teacher is doing what Friere (1983) calls "apprehending" – taking in and making meaning of the totality.

In order to comprehend more fully the need for and implications of good listening in interpersonal communication, it is helpful to go back in time and history, first, to the work of Carl Rogers, who distinguished himself as a "client-centered therapist" in the mid-twentieth century (Rogers, 1961). Rogers was among the first to write about the importance of "good communication skills" in effective interpersonal interactions. He raised awareness of how people listen – and pointed out those personal communication habits that detract from good listening, citing, first, our "very natural tendency to judge, evaluate, disapprove, approve" what another person is saying (Rogers, 1961, p. 330). Rogers noted that "although the tendency to make evaluations is common in almost all interchanges of language, it is very much heightened in those situations where feelings and emotions are deeply involved." Based on Rogers's work, it would appear that the very first step in developing good listening skills occurs when the tendency to evaluate and judge can be avoided so that we can listen with the purpose of understanding. That would include the ability to see a student's statement from that student's point of view, to "sense how it feels to him [sic] to achieve his [sic] frame of reference in regard to the thing he [sic] is talking about" (Rogers, 1961, p. 332). Rogers also pointed out, as many who have also studied "listening skills" in the interactive process, that this is far more difficult than it sounds. Although much has been written since about the importance of "good listening skills" and "active listening" in areas such as conflict resolution and counseling, much of what has appeared is little more than a restating of Rogers's original ideas (e.g., Fisher & Ury, 2012; Zenger & Folkman, 2016; Kyle, 2014).

Rogers cautioned us that to be become an effective listener – that is, to be able to truly and honestly put yourself into the place where you can free yourself from judging and listen, apprehending fully, and with compassion, to what a student is telling you, entering into his or her mind frame, getting at his or her meaning, and being able to re-state it in a way that demonstrates that you HAVE heard and understood – is a learned skill that requires some risk taking. Because if and when the teacher can effect such listening skills, free from the need to judge and evaluate, he or she is likely to "run the risk of being changed him/herself." Of course, Rogers means this in the best sense.

Another impediment occurs when the student is making a statement that has high emotionality – a statement that cuts into the heart of what the teacher believes, or cares deeply about. It is only when the teacher can put aside his or her own feelings that he or she can dispatch the need to judge and listen with truly "open ears." So before teachers proceed on their own development of good listening skills, it is best to be forewarned of these caveats – for to be aware and conscious of our own ability to listen and apprehend is the very first step in more effective skill development.

Based upon the original work of Rogers, Robert Carkhuff and his colleagues (2000) provided us with further insight into how people could be trained to become more effective in their interpersonal communications. His identification of the key ingredients of interpersonal communication skills put "listening and attending" at the top of his list. In his description of attending, he suggested that it involves communicating a hovering or undivided attentiveness to the person, focusing the teacher's observing and listening skills upon the student's verbal and non-verbal expressions of their experiences. Attending also serves to communicate an intense interest in the experiences of the students and so motivates them to become more involved in the interpersonal process (Carkhuff, 2000, p. 39).

The work done at the Graduate School of Business at Harvard, under the wise mentorship and teaching of C. Roland Christensen, has produced a network of resources that address the kind and quality of communication skills required for effective interactive teaching. Herman B. Leonard, Professor of Public Sector Finance Management in the JFK School of Government, summed it up by stating:

> Good listening – focused, critical, comprehensive, and strategic – requires discipline. A wide spectrum of messages can be conveyed through spoken communication, and the shades of meaning can be very subtle. Great concentration is needed to absorb, organize, and store verbal communication in a form that makes later retrieval both possible and useful. But if true discussion is to take place in the classroom, then all participants – teachers and students alike – must acquire perceptive listening skills. (Leonard, 1991, p. 140)

The strategies in what is sometimes called "active listening" (Olsen, 2016) include the teacher's ability to focus, with intensity, on the statement the student is making; "attend" with both eye contact and body language to the student as he or she is speaking; comprehend the verbal and non-verbal message that is being communicated; and allow for "wait time" to give the student sufficient opportunity to frame the statements and make the meanings clearer. Underlying all of this is the *a priori* condition of respect – that includes not only the teacher's full and undivided attention, but also the absence of judgment, in statement, tone, and overall behavior.

Adela Rosemarin (1985), in describing her impression of group discussions, highlights the fact that students' statements are sometimes not what they seem on the surface. "As in life, statements in class often carry many messages in addition to the obvious or denotative" (p. 36). With good listening skills, one can more easily discern not only the words that are being communicated, but also any underlying meanings. Getting to the deeper meanings of students' statements can lead to more productive examinations of the big ideas.

The teacher's overall behavior, in addition to the active listening, is also part of the message communicated to the student, demonstrating: "I hear you; I'm listening and attempting to understand what you are saying." Overall behavior is one important indicator of that active listening stance. For example, some teachers, even in very large classes, will move toward the student who is speaking, and address that student directly, eye-to-eye. Others move more closely, but do not directly "lean in" on the student. Some teachers move around the class – but few, if any, remain in a sitting or standing position without moving – the movement itself communicating a sense of "being with" the students as they are offering their ideas.

Listening, attending, and tuning in are not all one-sided affairs that benefit only the student. The teacher, in the process, is also an important beneficiary, for the ability to reach in, interpret and make meaning of students' statements can result in an enriched exchange of ideas, and discerning insights that build on each other. It also keeps the teacher close to what is going on. Teachers become role models for students – clearly demonstrating the value of good listening. And not least, the attention to individual students and their ideas tells them, explicitly and implicitly, that what they say has value and that you value them and their ideas. "You show them by example that discussion is predicated on respect for all contributions; and the most obvious token of respect is attentive listening" (Leonard, 1991, p. 146).

Now the Fun Begins

Many have heard the old warhorse about the guy on the corner of Broadway and 59th Street in New York City who asks a stranger, "How do you get to Carnegie Hall?" to which the answer is, "Practice, practice, practice." In learning any skills, there's no avoiding the arduous business of putting what one knows into practice, and refining those skills with practice, practice, and practice and reflection on practice. The bad news is that no one gets to Carnegie Hall without years of concentrated practice on one's instrument – unless one is Florence Foster Jenkins and has the money to rent the hall, and give out free passes to her friends. But no one said she could sing. One master's class student asked Segovia, the virtuoso classical guitarist, at age 80, what he did to become so expert in his art and was told, "My son, I never practice my scales more than 5 hours a day."

But the good news is that there are exercises to develop good listening skills – that help one become not only more expert, but also attain the ability to do that naturally, and without apparent effort. In other words, practice does help one to become not only skilled, but to attain mastery. In the process of developing this basic interactive skill, it may be helpful to remember the advice of Paul Winchell (1954) to trainees in ventriloquism:

> Don't rush.
> Don't get impatient.
> Don't get discouraged.
> Don't ever give up.

A Personal Training Program for Improving One's Listening and Attending Skills

In developing the basic listening and attending skills, the following guidelines may be helpful. Your ability to attend thoughtfully and perceive accurately – to apprehend – increases when the following conditions are met:

- You are able to make and hold eye contact with the student who is speaking.
- You are able to listen and to communicate verbal and non-verbal respect for the student's ideas.
- You are able to free yourself from the need to evaluate or judge the student's ideas, in either tone or word.
- You are able to avoid commenting on the student's idea reactively and/or presenting your own idea in rebuttal.

- You are able to make meaning of – to apprehend – what the student is saying.
- You have an awareness in tone of any affect (verbal or non-verbal) being communicated by the student.
- You are especially aware of indicators of stress being shown by the student.
- You can begin to paraphrase responses that accurately and sensitively reflect the meaning of the student's statement.
- You are able to make the student feel safe, non-defensive, and non-threatened throughout the interchange, through your verbal and non-verbal behavior.

Beginning with Role-Play Practice Tasks

The most comfortable way to begin working on listening and attending skills is – oddly – with simulations. Not exactly "in the pit" – but considerably less stressful and less challenging. The simulation is more comfortable as a beginning practice task – giving the teacher the benefit of working with a like-minded small group, free from the very active and more volatile actual classroom situation. Of course, vital elements of the reality are absent – but like practicing scales, which is not the same as making music, these simulations begin the process of listening as one "tries to hear" what is being said by the chosen partners in the simulation. It is not an actual classroom – but it is a beginning, a starting point. Another caveat is that the statements in the practice task are more often more clearly put – and in the real domain of human interactions, it is sometimes the case that a student will not be articulate and not able to express his or her ideas clearly. Sometimes, even students' good ideas may elude effective expression. So there is that. But a simulation is, after all, only the beginning.

Ideally, when beginning work on a simulation to practice listening and attending, the practice begins with trios – like-minded colleagues or friends, with one person playing the role of "teacher," one the "student," and one the "monitor." Obviously, the "student" is the one who makes a statement and the "teacher" the one who listens, attends, and attempts to paraphrase, or say back – indicating that he or she has "heard and understood." The "monitor" attends, and perhaps keeps notes, but more importantly, provides feedback to the "teacher" about the extent to which he or she has met the guidelines above. Each simulation should continue for about 5–10 minutes. Then, the roles are switched, so that each one in the trio has an opportunity to be student, teacher, and monitor. After each simulation, the practice task is "debriefed" and suggestions are made to the teacher and student, which may be incorporated in the next practice session. At this level of practice, the "teacher" is advised to listen and only to either paraphrase what has been heard, or to say back – repeating what has been heard. The result of this response is that the student has felt "heard" – and that his or her statement has been accepted and "played back" without judgment.

42 Listening, Attending, Apprehending, Making Meaning

Practice Tasks in Listening, Attending, Paraphrasing, and Being Non-Judgmental

Appendix A contains several suggestions for practicing listening, attending, paraphrasing, and being non-judgmental in simulations with like-minded colleagues. The practice tasks include suggestions for how to proceed, what to watch for, and how to debrief, in order to ensure that the process of skill development benefits from each trio's input into what needs further attention for the next practice. Lists of possible "student statements" have been included as suggestions for discussion – but they are far from the only issues that may be examined. Teachers should feel free to choose their own topics – giving special attention to those issues that are relevant and current to the teacher's concerns. Any topic is grist for the mill – with the proviso that it will, undoubtedly, be more difficult for neophytes to maintain a neutral stance on those topics that they are more passionate about.

Postgame Reflections on Simulations

Each simulation, each trio, should be followed up by discussion that reflects on the key issues of "listening, attending, waiting, being neutral." Some questions that can serve as guidelines to those discussions may be helpful – but it is important that each "player" participate in examining how the discussion was enabled by putting into practice the basic elements of discussion teaching.

1. To what extent did the "student" feel respected during the discussion? What was done to communicate that respect?
2. To what extent did the "student" feel listened to?
3. To what extent was the "teacher" able to tune in to the ideas being expressed by the "student?" What factors, if any, were seen to hinder this?
4. To what extent was the "teacher" aware of the non-verbal aspects of what the "student" was saying? What factors, if any, seemed to hinder this?
5. To what extent was the "teacher" aware of the "student's" feelings? Of signs of stress? And how effectively did the "teacher" respond to these signs?
6. To what extent was the "teacher" able to paraphrase, accurately, the "student's" statements? What responses are examples of this?
7. What was the effect of this simulation on the "student?" What response can the "student" make about this practice session? What advice can the "student" give to the "teacher?"
8. What would the "teacher" like to say about his or her interactions in this practice session?
9. What other comments would anyone like to make?

Conclusion

Sometimes, when undertaking a new methodology, or new strategies, it seems, at first, like swimming through glue – so much to learn and so far to go. Yet, the training of teachers as "discussion leaders" has netted huge payoffs, in terms of their increased skills, abilities, and understanding of the process. What's more, the results seen in their classrooms seem to be worth all of their efforts.

Leonard (1991, p. 150) has written that "listening is a profoundly human activity. It requires that we be sensitive to various strands of the messages we hear. It requires that we be conscious of the multiple dimensions of what people have to say. It affirms our respect for others as people, and for their ideas and contributions."

In the end, the good listener will find that this finely honed skill pays off in other arenas outside of the discussion classroom. It enables us to be more sensitively tuned to others in many aspects of our lives – not only to those "working through their issues" but also to those with whom we have ordinary dinner conversations. As we become good listeners, we become enablers in interpersonal communications – with whomever and wherever we are in conversation. It gives us the power and the tools to communicate to others that we understand them – their ideas, their issues, their feelings. And for many people, this is an enormous gift of facilitation.

References

Carkhuff, Robert R. (2000). *The Art of Helping*. Amherst: Human Resources Press.
Fisher, Roger, & Ury, William (2012). *Getting to Yes*. New York: Random House.
Friere, Paolo (1983). *Pedagogy of the Oppressed*. London: Continuum.
Kyle, Arnold (2014). "Behind the Mirror: Reflective Listening and Its Tain in the Work of Carl Rogers." *The Humanistic Psychologist*, 42(4), 354–369.
Leonard, Herman B. (1991). "With Open Ears: Listening and the Art of Discussion Leadership." In C. R. Christensen, David A. Garvin, & A. Sweet (eds.), *Education for Judgment: The Artistry of Discussion Leadership*. Boston: Harvard Business School Press, pp. 137–152.
Olsen, Christian. (2016). *Listening: Learn to Really Listen and Develop Active Listening Skills*. CreateSpace Independent Publishing Platform.
Rogers, Carl (1961). *On Becoming a Person*. Boston: Houghton Mifflin.
Rosmarin, Adela (1985). "The Art of Leading a Discussion." In Margaret M. Gullette (ed.), *On Teaching and Learning*. Boston: Harvard-Danforth Center for Teaching and Learning, pp. 34–39.
Winchell, Paul (1954). *Ventriloquism for Fun and Profit*. Baltimore: Ottenheimer.
Zenger, Jack, & Folkman, Joseph (2016). "What Great Listeners Actually Do." *Harvard Business Review*, July 14, 2016. https://hbr.org/product/what-great-listeners-actually-do/H030DC-PDF-ENG

6

BASIC INTERACTIVE SKILLS: RESPONDING, SAYING BACK, PARAPHRASING, INTERPRETING

A teacher's commitment to listen, attend and apprehend in response to what students are saying is the first step in the building of the interactive dialogue. This step sets the stage for what is to follow, while demonstrating to students that what they have said is of value and that it is being respectfully and non-judgmentally heard. It also gives teachers the information they need to think about an appropriate response to the student's statement – the two-way "exchange" that begins the interactive dialogue. Important in this process is the teacher's ability to comprehend what the student is trying to say – because, alas, as many teachers know, students may not be so articulate in expressing their ideas that their statements are so easily understood.

So if the student's meaning is elusive, the teacher may call for clarification. For example:

- Can you help me out, Wilhelm? I'm not sure I understood you.
- Frances, I'm going to try to say that back to you and you tell me if you think I've understood you correctly.

In these examples, it is clear that it is the teacher who assumes the responsibility of not understanding. The student is not made to feel stupid; it is the teacher who is missing the meaning. The student is not penalized; he or she is given another opportunity to help the teacher understand. For students, framing their ideas into comprehensible statements may be a matter of developing these skills. If that is the case, it surely follows that the more students are given practice in communicating their ideas clearly, the better they ought to get at communicating clearly.

When the teacher can fully grasp what the student is trying to say, this allows that teacher to formulate an appropriate response so that the interactive dialogue can continue on a productive course.

Waiting for Students to Express Their Ideas

The pressure on teachers to get everything done by the end of the school day, or class period, is palpable. That race with the clock puts a burden on teachers that forces them to speed up lessons, and lose patience with students who need more time to say what is on their minds. While I know that pressure intimately, and have had nightmares about students finishing the school year with still so much more I wanted to teach them left undone, I nonetheless am suggesting that students be given adequate time to think, to say what they mean and to say it clearly. Good ideas take time to "hatch." And we teachers cannot have it both ways. We cannot have quality of thinking and speed – they are antagonistic to each other. In conducting effective classroom discussions, where students are being asked to offer ideas, waiting for students to think about what they want to say and say it clearly must trump the rush to finish. In the end, teachers will have to choose which goal is the more important.

Being Non-Judgmental in Accepting Students' Responses: Appreciating Students' Ideas

How do students learn to be fearful of offering their ideas? And what are the strategies that make it safe for students to say what they think? We've known for many years that when students' ideas are being constantly judged as "right" or "wrong" they are less likely to volunteer them. It's been more than half a century since Rogers admonished that the major impediment in productive classroom discussion is teachers' very natural tendency to judge, to evaluate, and to approve or disapprove students' ideas (Rogers, 1961).

If students are fearful that their ideas are going to be condemned they are less likely to offer them. If students know that certain ideas are going to be rewarded, only those who are convinced they have "what the teacher wants to hear" will be the ones who volunteer them and those students will dominate the discussions. Students who are fearful of being penalized will rarely, if ever, participate. If a teacher has noted that classroom discussion is an activity in which only a small group of students carries on a private dialogue with the teacher while the rest of the class is tuned out, tweeting on their cell phones, a look at the teacher's judgmental responses may offer a clue to why this has occurred.

Some teachers still cling to the belief that telling students when they are right and wrong is a big part of the teacher's job. However, such evaluative utterances militate against a climate in which new and innovative ideas may flourish (Runco & Pritzker, 1999, p. 637). Once again, teachers cannot have it both ways; they cannot set themselves up as "idea critics" in which every student statement is judged, as well as create a climate in which all students' ideas are welcomed and treated with respectful attention. This may be asking a lot of teachers – to shed the critic's mantle and substitute, instead, responses like "I see" or "Tell me more, Jorge" or "Let me see if I've understood you, Shawana." However, the teacher who dares to step into this territory need only to put this element of effective classroom discussions to the test, in their own classrooms, to recognize the power of more facilitative responses, in place of judgment.

A teacher who avoids judging student statements as "good" or "right" or even "interesting" does not neglect to show appreciation for a student's contribution. Thus, "Thanks, Eva, for sharing your ideas with us" is not only acceptable, but a welcome part of a productive discussion. Of course, the bottom line in showing appreciation is the teacher's genuineness in offering it. Anything that sounds phony is counterproductive.

There may be times when a student's statement is so "off the wall" that a teacher may be non-plussed. For example:

> STUDENT: Well, I think that children who commit serious crimes should be punished as adults.
> TEACHER: Punishment should be the same for kids as for adults.
> STUDENT: Yeh. Do the crime, do the time.
> TEACHER: You'd extend that penalty to kids of all ages – maybe down to five-year-olds.
> STUDENT: No, I don't think five-year-olds. But older.
> TEACHER: Maybe ten-year-olds.
> STUDENT: I'm not sure.
> TEACHER: You're not sure of the cut-off point for an age group to receive punishment as adults – but you think that five and ten may be too young.

Tamping down the urge to call an idea crazy, an interactive dialogue that requires the student to examine his or her statement can be much more productive than a judgment that condemns the idea and implicitly condemns the student.

Conditions that Limit and Actually Crush Student Thinking

A discussion about the important elements of effective interactive teaching is incomplete without giving some voice to a few other threads of the interactive process – those conditions that limit and, worse, crush student thinking. As much as we'd like to believe otherwise, when such stifling of students' thinking is the major mode of teacher–student interactions, students' abilities to voice their ideas and to think intelligently about what they want to say dries up, like so many autumn leaves (Wassermann, 2009).

There is an abundance of data to suggest that when teachers agree or disagree with students' statements, those kinds of responses "put paid" to student thinking processes. There is no requirement to think further. Rushing through a lesson without giving students a chance to think is another way in which teachers limit opportunities to think. ("No matter what I do in the Civil War unit, Grant has to be in Richmond by Thanksgiving!")

The teacher who tells students what they think also denies students the chance to think for themselves, to generate their own ideas. When the teacher talks too much, explains things his or her way, gives information, or tells students what to think, all of these seemingly innocuous responses seriously curtail opportunities for students to exercise their own brain power.

More serious offenses are seen when a teacher cuts a student off, when he or she heckles or puts down a student's idea, or when the teacher responds sarcastically and belittles a student's responses. Teachers who resort to such modes of interaction make students fearful of thinking and therefore all motivation to offer their ideas is crushed. Of course, teachers do not use these responses with malice, but rather out of habit or a misguided belief that they are helpful rather than harmful. Bringing such an interactive style into the full light of day, and learning to listen and to monitor what is coming out of one's mouth, is the burden of any teacher who is committed to the idea that effective group discussions that emphasize students' abilities to generate their own ideas and express them clearly is an essential component of the art of discussion teaching.

Before launching into the "how" of formulating effective responses in an interactive dialogue, a few caveats need to be added to this discussion.

First, it is important to note that the key elements of interactive teaching are not seen every single moment of every teaching day. There are times when teachers will want to offer their own ideas. ("I think that we all need to pitch in and help someone out who is having difficulty.") There are times when a teacher will want to make an evaluative comment to a student who has done an exceptionally fine job. ("Mona, I loved your story. It was so touching it brought tears to my eyes.") There are times when a teacher will want students to know the important issues that led to the Civil War, addition facts and multiplication tables, different points of view about global warming, how to balance a checkbook, how to prepare a resume. And there are times when teachers will agree or disagree with a student, provide information, or explain certain procedures. The goal is, of course, to bring teaching strategies into synch with the teacher's goals for the lessons. There is a time for productive interactive discussions, in which the objective is to promote students' intelligent habits of mind with discussion teaching. And there are times for other kinds of responses. The art of discussion teaching, and, in fact, the art of teaching, is for the teacher to be clear about his or her goals, and use those teaching strategies that are in concert with those goals – consistently connecting our means with our ends.

Becoming Aware of Differences in Responding

In an interactive discussion, when the teacher has listened and apprehended the student's statement, there are several kinds of "basic" responses that will do the job of "clarifying" the student's thinking. Some responses serve to put the student's idea under examination by paraphrasing, or saying back. These communicate to the student that the teacher is listening, has heard, and wants to know if s/he has "heard correctly." "Saying back" does not wander far afield from the student's statement. It attends to and accurately reflects the student's idea by capturing the key words of the student's statement. The "saying back" is not done mechanically, but naturally. It is always respectful. Although this response does not contain the ingredients to move the discussion forward, it is, nonetheless, a productive way of helping the student to hear the idea played back and to think about what he or she has said. For example:

> STUDENT: When they build houses all alike like those in the photo, it's so boring!
> TEACHER: When houses look all alike, you find that pretty dull.

A paraphrase departs a bit more from the student's statement. In paraphrasing, the teacher takes a minimal risk in using words or phrases that might misinterpret the student's meaning. However, when the paraphrased response accurately captures the student's meaning, it enables the student to work with his or her idea, and come to a deeper understanding of the implications of the statement. For example:

> STUDENT: When they build houses all alike like those in the photo, it's so boring!
> TEACHER: When the houses in a community are all alike, it seems a very uninteresting place to live.

A teacher may also interpret what the student is saying. In interpreting, the teacher "reads into" the student's statement considerably more than what has actually been said. Good interpreting requires the most thoughtful and accurate attending, as the teacher risks making an inaccurate interpretation. When the interpretation is accurate, it brings a new element into the discussion for the student to consider, and allows the student to gain new insights into his or her thinking. For example:

> STUDENT: When they build houses all alike like those in the photo, it's so boring!
> TEACHER: A community where all the houses are built on exactly the same model seems very unappealing to you. It says something to you about the people who would choose to live there.

Responses that interpret may also include "reading into" non-verbal behavior and affect. For example:

> STUDENT: When they build houses all alike like those in the photo, it's so boring!
> TEACHER: Living there would hardly be the place of your dreams. If the houses are so boring, what would the people be like!

A teacher may also ask for more information. This is done when the teacher wants the student to elaborate, to say a little more about his or her idea. For example:

> TEACHER: What was different about the missionaries' and the natives' ways of life?
> STUDENT: Houses.
> TEACHER: Say a little more about that, Celeste.

These are some of the "basic" responses that are safe, probe gently, and rarely put the student at risk. There is no hard and fast rule for which response to use and when, but it has been my experience to begin with simple paraphrasing, setting the tone and the manner and building to slightly more challenging responses, like interpreting and asking for examples. If there were rules to apply, it would make interactive teaching easy! But like my grandmother, who when baking bread used only her eyes and hands to "feel" when the dough was ready, the more experienced teacher will learn to "feel" or sense when to begin digging more deeply into what the student is thinking and saying. The best rule of thumb in this is to tread softly and gently, moving ahead when it seems safe to do so, keeping eyes and ears "tuned in" to the verbal and non-verbal behavior of the students and using these as cues to the next responses. There is no getting around the notion that students will feel more unsafe when the teacher probes more deeply into what the student is thinking, requiring the student to defend his or her ideas; that is why it is helpful to remember that paraphrasing is not only the safest response, but also a productive one.

Some responses call for deeper analyses, putting the student at greater cognitive risk. These are not used at first, but only when the teacher–student interchange has built up a head of steam. These responses ask if assumptions have been made, or if what the student believes is "good," or if the student has considered alternatives, or if there are data that support the student's ideas. These latter responses may be stated as questions, but they can also be made safer by framing them as statements. For example, rather than "What assumptions have you made, Joshua?" a teacher can soften it by saying, "Joshua, I wonder if you've made some assumptions here?" Or a teacher can soften "Have you thought a lot about that, Sherman?" by saying, "Sherman, I see you've been giving that a lot of thought." A question that sounds like an interrogation, e.g., "Did you vote for Patsy?" can be softened by asking, "I'm wondering about how you made your decision to vote for Patsy." Like learning to knead bread, it's all in the wrist!

Appendix B offers three sets of practice tasks that provide experience at the grass-roots level of "listening, attending, and responding" to students' statements. In the first set of practice tasks, you are asked to "listen" and attend to a student's statement and then to formulate a paraphrase response that captures the student's meaning and "plays it back" to him or her. In the second set of practice tasks, you will be adding the dimension of interpreting the student's statement – providing a little more substance in asking the student to think about dimensions of his or her ideas, and taking the ideas to deeper levels of understanding and meaning. The first two sets of practice tasks are written exercises. In the third set, you begin to use the interactive responses in role-play simulations that are recorded and analyzed.

By way of example, here's a brief transcript of a teacher's interactions with a young student:

> CARMEN: Bees get their honey from the flowers.
> TEACHER: The honey is in the flowers and the bees get it from the flowers. (Paraphrase)
> CARMEN: Yeh.
> TEACHER: Tell me a little more about how that works. (Asks for clarification)
> CARMEN: They go to the flower and suck the honey out.
> TEACHER: So the honey is in the flower. (Interprets)
> CARMEN: No, they make the honey. It's not in the flower.
> TEACHER: The bees make the honey with something they take from the flower. (Paraphrase)
> CARMEN: They get syrup from the flower and they make honey from the syrup.
> TEACHER: It's the flowers that have syrup and the bees use that syrup to make honey.
> (Paraphrases)
> CARMEN: Yeh.
> TEACHER: How do they do that, I wonder? Do you have any ideas about it? (Asks for more information; clarification)

Self-assessment

In learning new strategies, new methods, new music, new ways of making Crepe Suzette, it is not enough to practice, practice, practice. Because as anyone knows who has attempted to try a Beethoven sonata, practice alone does not necessarily help one improve. One must learn to listen to what is being practiced, and to make the corrections necessary for the subsequent practice sessions. If we don't learn to listen to what we are practicing and "hear" where we are playing wrong notes, or using the wrong fingering, or playing forte, when the music calls for piano, then we fall into the habit of practicing the wrong notes again and again (Britzman, 2003). So learning to listen to oneself, without defensiveness, is a vital part of developing and building new skills.

Donald Schoen called this "reflection in action" and "reflection on action" – the first, the ability to tune into self while in the act of teaching (Schoen, 1983); the second, the ability to reflect back on what was done or said, and use that as material to make corrections in the next practice session. These are the higher level skills that are called for in the process of developing expertise – requiring that we drop our defensiveness, see and hear ourselves in the harsh, cruel light of how we really are when we are in error, and accept those errors as working material to improve. The more defensiveness can be dropped, as not only an impediment, but as a true obstacle to growth, the greater the chances for developing mastery.

It's helpful to begin, at first, with a debriefing of the work in the role-play simulations, using, as a guide, the Task Analysis materials found in Appendix D. If all of the "players" work together to build a cooperative ethos, helping, pointing out tactfully and gracefully, where the faults are to be found and making recommendations for the next round – such debriefings among friends and colleagues can be very useful. At the very next level, you might consider using your iPhone or other video-recording device to make a video record of your work in the role-play simulations and, in the safety of your own room, sit back, watch and learn, again using the Task Analysis materials as a guide to examine your interactions, making special notes of where you need to focus for your next trials.

Alas, there is no way around such self-examination – done, at first, with friends or colleagues, and then, on one's own. Like looking into a mirror, and examining all our warts – the good news is that eventually you will become more practiced, more skillful and more masterful in your interactive dialogues.

References

Britzman, Deborah P. (2003). *Practice Makes Practice*. New York: SUNY Press.
Rogers, Carl (1961). *On Becoming a Person*. Boston: Houghton Mifflin.
Runco, Mark A., & Pritzker, Steven R. (eds.) (1999). *Encyclopedia of Creativity, Vol. 1*. San Diego: Academic Press.
Schoen, Donald (1983). *The Reflective Practitioner*. San Francisco: Jossey-Bass.
Wassermann, Selma (2009). *Teaching for Thinking Today*. New York: Teachers College Press.

7

BASIC INTERACTIVE SKILLS: QUESTIONING[1]

Good questions are a teacher's stock in trade. Used wisely, they can reach into a student's mind to get at the surface and undercurrents of a student's thinking. Used wisely, they can enable a student's examination of not only what he or she has been thinking, but also how he or she has arrived at those ideas. Used wisely, they can correct errors in judgment, spot false assumptions, and bring about a critical examination of the data that have been used to form ideas. Used wisely, they can bring about reflection on beliefs that lead to behavior. Used wisely, they can slice through the thin membrane of "magical thinking" that belies rationality and leads to ill-informed decisions. Used wisely, they are a powerful tool in a teacher's repertoire of interactive skills. The key words in the art of asking good questions are "used wisely." Because questions cannot only illuminate and generate critical thinking, but used inappropriately, can lead to a shutting down of thinking and a raising of students' levels of defensiveness.

The goal of good questions is to promote reflection, rather than to interrogate; to allow for student responses that lead to continued examination of the big ideas; and to invite, rather than command. They are clear in what they ask students to think about and not so broad or abstract that they defeat the process of thoughtful examination. There is much more to asking good questions than merely making interrogative demands. If an interactive dialogue is to bear fruit, so that students may examine issues intelligently, questions must be sensitive to many aspects of the interactive process. These include an awareness of how questions are articulated, as well as how they are voiced, so that they do not provoke undue anxiety and defensiveness. The question most often heard in classrooms is "Why?" – which is, perhaps, the most aggressive form of putting a student on the spot. Learning to shed facile questions, reframing them to obtain the best results, knowing which kinds of questions to use and when to use them, and knowing the difference between different kinds of questions and their potential for generating the best quality of student thinking is the heart of this chapter.

The road to asking more productive questions is not always a smooth one. Teachers who initiate these kinds of questions into classroom discussions are likely to meet student resistance initially, since students who have been programmed to respond with single correct answers may balk at having to think their own ideas and use their minds in more challenging ways. For students who have lived their school lives in the black and white world of certainty, productive questions, which elevate ambiguity and uncertainty, are likely to create higher levels of dissonance and anxiety. Yet, the payoff for using productive questions is rich. Effectively used, they build habits of thinking; they give students practice in reasoning from the data, in arguing a point of view, in examining issues from more than one perspective, in differentiating between fact and opinion. If these learning goals are important to teachers, they will doubtless find creative and skillful ways to help students bridge the gap from initial resistance to more rewarding behaviors. Experience with the process tells us that once students have crossed that bridge, once they have tasted the freedom of thinking for themselves, there is no going back.

One important skill in the art of questioning requires teachers to understand the differences between questions that promote examination and those that call for recall of information, i.e., for teachers to be clear in what they are asking of the student. Does the teacher want to know what students know, or how they use what they know to achieve understanding? The two purposes require different kinds of questions.

Also important is that questions be selectively used in an interactive dialogue because when a question is asked, it has the force of shifting the discussion onto a new, but related issue. An overuse of questions would result in a dialogue that would be constantly shifting focus, like the ragged edge of a torn fabric. An effective interactive dialogue would normally consist of many types of responses, including paraphrasing, interpreting, saying back and asking for examples, as well as questioning. (Examples of such dialogues are found in Chapter 8.) Questions are raised when the teacher senses that it is time for the discussion to move on, as they will open new doors for examination. The teacher is in the "driver's seat" – listening, attending, and with a sensitive ear, deciding when the discussion needs a question to probe more deeply into the big ideas. There are no hard and fast rules for this; but an awareness of the results of the interactive dialogue will give evidence of the productivity of the examination. And of course, reflection-on-action will provide the teacher with a perspective on the responses he or she has used and how effective they were in producing the results that were hoped for. It was Professor Christensen, in a private conversation with the author, who said, "When a class discussion has gone badly, I am awake all night thinking about what I might have said differently. And when a class discussion has gone well, I am awake all night thinking about what I did to produce those results." So, yes, there is no free lunch.

The identification of different types of questions described in the following paragraphs is merely the introduction to effective practice. Using this understanding to sharpen one's interactive teaching skills is what master teachers spend the rest of their teaching lives learning and polishing.

Unproductive Questions

There are several categories of unproductive questions that do little or nothing to promote thoughtful examination of ideas. In some of the worst instances, they are hurtful and they humiliate. Others dismiss students' ideas, implicitly suggesting that they have no value. There are undoubtedly other categories of unproductive questions, but what follows are examples of those types of questions that are not only useless for promoting thinking, but also may be psychologically harmful.

Stupid Questions

This is a harsh way to identify a category of questions – but truth to be told, each and every one of us has heard his and her share of them. And because they so often do more harm than provide information sought, it may not be a disservice to label them as Carkhuff has done (2000).

Stupid questions, by and large, may be frequently heard from the lips of interviewers on television news. "How did you feel when the earthquake destroyed all the homes in your neighborhood?" asked the well-intentioned, beautifully coiffed woman with the microphone. Such a question is not only insulting to the person or people who have been devastated by the loss of their homes, their property, and everything they cared about, but it also makes the observer cringe. Insensitive, disrespectful, thoughtless – they trivialize what is emotionally and intellectually complex.

What is the answer to a question like that? "Oh, I was scared." We learn nothing from the response that we had not known before. Of course people are scared when an earthquake strikes. What did we expect? Suddenly the question becomes more than stupid. It reduces to banality what is terrifying and horrifying. TV news interviews are not the only place where stupid questions are heard. However, the example serves as an introduction to the discussion about stupid questions.

There are three conditions that identify stupid questions: (1) The question does not attend to the student's idea. (2) The question is insensitive to the feelings or ideas being expressed. (3) The question is irrelevant or disrespectful.

Stupid questions have cognitive as well as affective consequences. At the cognitive level, they prohibit meaningful examination of the student's ideas. At the affective level, they implicitly communicate that the student's statement is without value. Through the question, the teacher shifts the focus of the discourse from the student's concern to the teacher's. This is not to suggest that teachers never shift the pathway of the dialogue from the student's idea to one the teacher considers more important; however, there are more respectful ways of doing this than by asking stupid questions.

Some examples of stupid questions overheard in educational contexts:

> STUDENT: My mother is very sick and they think she might die.
> TEACHER: How old is she?
> STUDENT: The volunteers on the beaches worked hard to try to save the birds, but they couldn't. They were covered with oil from the tanker spill.
> TEACHER: So how can we stop pollution?
> STUDENT: My neighborhood is so dangerous. There have been 8 homicides in the last six months. I'm afraid to walk outside.
> TEACHER: Where do you live?
> STUDENT: It's big money that corrupts the entire electoral process and subverts democracy.
> TEACHER: Did you vote?

Teachers' responses that are more respectful of each of the student's ideas above, and that enable more productive examination of the ideas, are often best framed as declarative sentences, rather than questions. For example, a better response to the student worried about his mother might be: "You're mom is dangerously ill and you are very worried about her." To the student worried about the effect of oil spills on marine life, a response might be: "You are so concerned about all those birds that were covered by the oil spill from the tanker. You have begun to see the effects of that pollution on the marine life in the area." A teacher who wants to encourage further examination of dangerous neighborhoods and homicides might respond: "The homicides in your neighborhood are out of control and out of proportion to the rest of the city. You are worried about being outside. There doesn't seem to be any end to them."

Questions that Are Too Complex

Another group of unproductive questions are those whose reach lies beyond a student's ability to respond intelligently within the scope of an interactive discussion. These "too big" questions tend to call for the examination of very sophisticated and complex issues; however, the questions themselves defeat such thoughtful examination. It is difficult to make an intelligent response, in a brief interaction, to the question, "What were the causes of World War I?"

The counterproductive underside to such questions is that they are asked by teachers and heard by students as calls for single, brief, and unambiguous answers. Through such questions and answers, students learn that there are quite simple answers for incredibly complex issues and they also learn to be satisfied with such simplicity even as adults.

Some examples of questions that are too complex for an interactive discussion are:

- Why is there pollution?
- What was the cause of the American Revolution?
- Why is there terrorism?
- Why are people prejudiced?

The ideas contained in these questions may be examined more productively by narrowing their focus. This not only makes them more manageable but implicitly cultivates the need for caution, openness and uncertainty in responding. For example:

- Tell us what you know about some of the ways in which pollution occurs.
- What were some of the conditions that led to the Colonists' discontent with British rule? Perhaps followed by: What do you suppose it takes to mobilize a group of people such as these Colonists to revolt against their legitimate rulers?
- What hypotheses can you suggest to explain what provokes a person to become a terrorist?
- What, in your experience, are some examples of prejudice? Perhaps to be followed by: How do you explain that behavior? What are your ideas?

Teacher-Answered Questions

Another group of unproductive questions are those that a teacher leaps to answer before students can respond. It is not that the questions themselves are not good. They are unproductive because no student is given time to think about an intelligent response. Many teachers use these liberally in their discussions. Perhaps their intentions are to get the students to think; but students have learned that if they do not respond within a few seconds, the teacher will provide the answer. There is no need for students to think. The teacher does it for them. There is no need for students even to listen. The teacher is carrying on a monologue.

- So how come the Indians grew corn? (pause) No one? Well, it's because the land was particularly suited to growing corn.
- How do we classify frogs? (pause) Amphibians, right?
- What were some of the reasons for the westward movement? (pause) OK. I'll give you a clue. Land. Right? There was all that land out there, and people were beginning to feel the need for more space.

It is fairly easy to solve this questioning problem. Mary Budd Rowe (1973) suggests "wait time," – that is, learning to wait (and wait and wait) until a student responds. Stahl (1994) also refers to "wait time" and "think time" as strategies that not only enable thoughtful examination of ideas, but lead to positive outcomes. One chemistry teacher taught himself to put his hands behind his back and count off seconds on his fingers. Before he got through counting, at least one student would break the silence. In that way, the teacher encourages the interactive dialogue to begin.

Trick Questions

Trick questions are deliberately (and sometimes maliciously) constructed to stump students. They are intended not only to show students up as pathetically inept, but also to show off the "smarts" of the teacher. When students cannot answer the trick question, the teacher waits and waits. Sometimes during this waiting period, the teacher will interject a derogatory comment to point up students' stupidity: "I'm surprised at you for not knowing that!"

While trick questions may serve momentarily to bolster a teacher's ego, the price for such cruelty is heavy. These teachers gain neither student respect nor admiration. In fact, students see these teachers for what they actually are: small persons who are trying to make themselves large at students' expense.

Questions that Humiliate

This category refers to questions that are laced with sarcasm, with inappropriate humor, with overt rejection, with negative judgment about the student's ability. It is hard to believe that teachers would deliberately set out to humiliate and degrade students. To give them the benefit of the doubt, perhaps these are misguided attempts to get students to "pull up their socks" and do good work. Yet, however well-intentioned, questions that are full of sarcasm and rejection are so wounding, so utterly destructive, that students who experience them carry scars long afterwards. How else would graduate students at university learn to preface their questions in seminar with the self-protective introduction, "This may be a stupid question, but …"

Even to read them from the printed page is to wince; yet these questions have been heard from teachers:

- How come you don't know that? Is your memory that short?
- It's green? You think it's green?? How on earth did you come up with that idea?
- Come on now. Even you can answer this one, can't you?
- This is so easy, a ten-year-old could do it. How come you can't?

The intention of such questions is not to promote thoughtful examination of ideas, but rather to bring students up short, to expose their ignorance to public view. No student comes away unscathed from such an encounter. The effect is a diminishing of confidence, which, for some students, is a deeply crushing blow, from which they are unable to recover any time soon. For some students, it means never again speaking out in class, if they can help it.

Less-than-Productive Questions

Some questions may call for students to examine ideas, but the way they are stated defeats more productive examination. These questions may fall short because they deal with trivia instead of important issues, because they are too difficult for the students, or because their wording is ambiguous. With a shift of phrase, or focus, less-than-productive questions can become more generative.

Trivial Questions

Trivial questions do not call on students to examine issues of substance. Often, these questions miss the meaning of what is important in the student's statement. The following examples of trivial questions come from a kindergarten classroom discussion on which animals would make good pets:

> CAMERON: A parrot would make a good pet because it has a big tongue and it can talk.
> TEACHER: How did you find out the parrot had a tongue?
> BRIAN: Elephants would make good pets because they could stomp on robbers, if robbers came to your house.
> TEACHER: What else could elephants do?

Put differently, these questions might zero in on what was important in the discussion about pets. For example: "Do you suppose there is something about a parrot's tongue that makes it possible for it to talk? What do you think?" Or, "You think elephants could make good pets. I wonder if you know anyone who has an elephant for a pet? How come, do you suppose?"

Questions that Are Too Abstract

Questions that are too abstract defeat thoughtful examination. They may be worded in such a way that they are not easily understood. Or they may reach beyond students' levels of experience and beyond what they are able to comprehend. Such questions may appear, at first, to be challenging, but usually result in inappropriate answers, or worse, no answers.

To ask a six-year-old, "How does an image get on an videotape?" is an example of a question that is too abstract and beyond the conceptual grasp of a six-year-old. Other abstract questions include such humdingers as:

- Why do people litter?
- How do birds learn to fly?
- How do magnets get their power?

These questions are, of course, "answerable" in some fashion by even the inexperienced student. (e.g.,"Birds learn to fly by natural instinct.") However, if the teacher's purpose is to further examination and understanding of the big ideas, questions framed in the following ways are likely to yield more productive responses:

- What can you tell me about how all the candy wrappers and orange peels end up on our schoolyard, instead of in the baskets?
- How do you suppose birds learn to fly? What ideas do you have about it?
- You have observed how magnets have the power to attract and repel. Tell us about some of your observations.

When a more abstract question is phrased as a request for hypotheses, this brings it down to a lower level of abstraction. In that way, students may respond from observations rooted in their experiences, building habits of thinking and giving way to more intelligent examination of the big ideas.

Ambiguous Questions

Questions may be ambiguous because they are poorly worded, resulting in confusing the student. Ambiguous questions may also occur because the teacher lacks practice in formulating precisely worded questions, or if he or she feels under stress. When the language of the question is unclear, or when the intent of the question is misunderstood, student responses may be understandably inept with respect to the issues under examination. Some examples of ambiguous questions are:

- What kinds of things did you come up with that you felt were going to be important for constructing your paper airplane?
- Why did the ancient Greeks have a good culture?

Framing questions clearly and unambiguously requires thinking about how the question might be stated before asking it. While such consideration may take an extra moment or two of the teacher's time, that extra moment may be a good investment if it yields more thoughtful student responses.

Hit-and-Run Questions

Hit and run questions are part of some teachers' style – the objective being to keep the discussion moving. Here, speed in question and answer takes precedence over the slower tempo of thoughtful examination of issues. Questions that come in a rapid-fire assault and flit from issue to issue, without allowing for connections to be made and without allowing for productive examinations, are ineffective in bringing about the results of intelligent habits of thinking.

The following is an example of a hit-and-run question sequence from a third-grade science lesson:

> TEACHER: What kind of water is in the ocean?
> ZACH: Salt.
> TEACHER: Salt water. Right. Now how do we get fresh water?
> ALLY: We could get it from the rain.
> TEACHER: Okay. So the rain is going to be fresh water. But how would we get the rainwater?
> FIONA: Clouds.
> TEACHER: But it would just fall to the ground. How would you get some?
> FIONA: In a cup.
> TEACHER: Okay. We could have a cup or bowl. Is there any other way of getting fresh water?
> JASON: Take some salt water and put it on a stove and boil it.
> TEACHER: When we boil it, it's going to be fresh water?
> JASON: Yeh.
> TEACHER: Nicole disagrees with you.
> NICOLE: I tried that once, but it still tasted salty.

Teachers who recognize the hit-and-run pattern in their interactive dialogue may wish to consider some of the ideas in the next sections in order to help shift their questioning and responding strategies away from the superficial toward examinations of matters of depth and substance.

Productive Questions

There are some questions that make the mind buzz, some that are so provocative that they continue to dwell in the mind for years. These questions keep us thinking, searching for understanding. They are questions of magnitude, provoking examination of ideas worth knowing and thinking about. They are particularly nettlesome because they are rarely rooted in certainty. It is the very reason they make us think. ("Does a cell have freedom of choice?")

If such questions cause so much trouble, why are they classified as productive? The two dimensions of troublesomeness and productivity are not, as one might expect, at odds. Productivity is borne out of troublesomeness; the creation of something new emerges from mental labor. We cannot give birth to an idea, create, or invent without putting the mind through labor.

Productive questions insist on the generation of something new. Whether the mind uses data to make analyses, as in comparing, classifying, or interpreting, or whether it is called on to leap from the data into brand new thought, as in suggesting hypotheses, creating, or evaluating, the mind is being challenged to bring forth new meanings, new configurations, new ideas. Since this is done in the absence of an absolute standard of right and wrong, such thoughts are left to dance in the great, uncharted territory of uncertainty. Nothing new can ever emerge from the certainty of what is already known.

Nothing new or of consequence occurs when students are asked the question: "Who painted the Mona Lisa?" But consider what may be uncovered if the question is put more productively: "As you observe this painting, what, in your view, contributes to its ranking as an art treasure?"

No new ideas emerge from the question, "What was the name of the group of people who landed at Plymouth Rock?" But consider what may be examined, instead, with a question that takes the learner down a more productive pathway: "What do you suppose were some of the very first experiences the Pilgrims had when they landed at Plymouth Rock in 1619? What data are you using to support your ideas?"

As in most matters of what happens in classrooms, it is the teacher who makes the choice that dictates the kinds of questions asked of students. And teachers will invariably make choices depending on personal needs and educational beliefs. If the teacher needs students to know the right answers, then no amount of persuasion is likely to influence their choice of questions that have clear and prescribed answers. Needs are not amenable to logical argument, nor are they negotiable. If teachers believe or may be persuaded to believe in the value of generative thinking, and if their needs do not constrain them from teaching in that muddy marshland of the unknown, it is likely that such teachers may choose the route of more productive questions.

Guidelines for Productive Questions

For teachers who want to use more productive questions in their interactive discussions, the guidelines below may be helpful.

Questions that Ask Students to Think More Generatively About Issues of Substance Are Drawn from the Higher Order Mental Operations

These include comparing, observing, classifying, hypothesizing, interpreting data, evaluating, deciding, creating, applying principles to new situations, and others (Bloom, 1956; Raths et al., 1986; Wassermann, 2009). These operations may be explicitly stated within the questions:

- What observations have you made about the way Matisse uses shapes in this painting?
- How would you compare the production of Stephen Sondheim's *Sweeney Todd* to a classical opera?
- How does the American Revolution compare with the French Revolution? What are some important differences? What are some similarities?

- What hypotheses can you suggest to explain some reasons for the British to have voted to leave the European Common Market?
- In making your choice of whom to vote for in a class election, what are some factors that influence your decision?
- What do you consider to be positive changes in lives that were brought about by the Industrial Revolution? What are some of your ideas about that?

On the other hand, the operations may not be explicitly stated, but instead may be implied in the question:

- What is your understanding of the events that led to the Great Depression of the 1930s? (interpreting data)
- How does the geography of the Andes bear on the climate, the living conditions, the culture, the politics, and the economics of Peru? (hypothesizing)
- Which character in the story would you choose for a friend? (evaluating, deciding)
- What do you suppose is meant by the phrase coined by P.T. Barnum, "There's a sucker born every minute?" (interpreting, evaluating)
- What, in your view, makes the Harry Potter books so popular? (evaluating, criticizing)

The Clearly Stated Question Makes It Easier for Students to Understand What Is Being Asked of Them

This requires a conscious effort in framing the question, hard enough to do in writing, but even harder to do in the heat of the moment. When teachers think that students are answering questions that are different from what the teacher thought was asked, it may be helpful to re-examine the language construction of the question. The good news is that the more teachers are conscious of the clarity demanded of questions, and the more they work on developing this skill, the easier it gets.

A Question that Has a Clear Focus Enables Students to Respond More Productively

One key to formulating well-focused questions is the teacher's clarity about what is to be examined in the question. In focusing the question, it is helpful to ask: What is it that I want the student to think about? On what issues (big ideas) do I want to focus with this question? This requires teachers to make choices about what's important in the examination of the big ideas. Here is an example of how this would work:

The students in a social studies class have examined the following chart comparing salaries of different professionals:

Average Salaries of Some Professionals in the U.S. in 2001–2002	
a. Teachers in Iowa	$38,230
b. Manny Ramirez (Boston Red Sox ballplayer)	$20,000,000
c. President of the U.S.	$400,000

If the teacher chooses to focus on the big ideas of unequal allocations of salaries for different groups of professionals, he/she might use that as a focus for the following types of questions:

- What observations can you make about the differences in pay for these professionals?
- How do you explain these differences in wages? What hypotheses can you suggest that might explain it?
- What observations can you make from the data about the professional who is most valued in terms of salary by us? How do you explain it?

The same, or another teacher, using the same chart, might choose to focus on the big ideas of how the public values these professionals in terms of their salaries:

- How, in your view, are these monetary values determined?
- Why do you suppose teachers earn so much less than baseball players? How do you explain that?
- How do salaries equate with our value of these professionals? What are your ideas about that?

The Question that Invites, Rather than Intimidates, Makes It Safer for Students to Give Their Best Thoughts

Tone of voice, nuance of expression, the communication of a mutual search for meaning, and the words that are used all contribute to the "feel" of the question. In attempting to frame questions as invitations to respond, it is helpful to think about whether you are asking the student to join you in the examination of this issue.

If the question is offered as an invitation to join in exploration, students are likely to feel a lot safer in generating ideas. If the question contains a hidden hook on which the student is going to be impaled, if it seems threatening or hostile, or if it seems disrespectful, the students' anxiety level may thwart an intelligent response. If a teacher has a specific answer in mind for the question, which is revealed by tone of voice, then this will alert students that it is unsafe for them to respond with their own ideas, that they are safe only if they come up with the idea that the teacher is seeking.

Productive Questions Make a Demand on Students to Think About Important Issues

Thoughtful reflection is significantly different from coming up with answers. It requires consideration of the issue and examination of data, alternatives, and examples – in short, the suspension of judgment and the elevation of ambiguity. Student thinking about issues is provoked when questions call for comparisons to be made, for observations, for setting up classifications, for evaluating and judging, for making choices, for interpreting data, and for applying principles to new situations.

Questions that call for thoughtful reflection include such examples as:

- What, in your view, explains the appeal of Mr. Donald Trump, the Republican elected president in the United States in the 2016 election?
- What do you see as some advantages of the parliamentary system of government? What arguments would you use to support a parliamentary system in the United States?
- What, in your view, makes for a compelling novel? How do your ideas relate to the overwhelming success of the Harry Potter books?

Questions that Are Respectful of Students' Feelings and Opinions Create a Climate of Trust, in Which They Feel Safer in Offering Their Ideas

The tone of a question reveals a teacher's underlying attitude towards students. If a teacher is respectful of students, sees them as partners in inquiry, and is comfortable in a non-judgmental role, then students will be more likely to respond to questions as invitations to examine issues thoughtfully. On the other hand, if a teacher has an attitude that speaks clearly as to who is in control and who has all the answers, then the teacher's questions are likely to reveal this and students will be more reluctant to risk offering their own views.

In examining the issue of respect for students, it is helpful to ask: Am I inviting students to examine ideas in a forum of true inquiry? Am I able to free myself from an authority role when responding to students' ideas and opinions? Am I able to avoid making positive or negative judgments about the responses given?

Questions that Require Students to Show How They Reason from the Data Allow Them to Use What They Know in Order to Understand Important Concepts

Questions that merely determine what students can recall will neither enliven discussion nor allow for examination of ideas. While it is certainly valuable to know certain pieces of information, these pieces become useful when we can put them to work for us. Putting them to work means being able to jiggle them around cognitively, to sort and process them, so that they reveal meaning and that connections can be made.

When asking productive questions, teachers do not abandon their charge to inform students and build their knowledge base. However, they put the emphasis on using knowledge to arrive at understanding. So instead of, "Who are the chief characters in the play Macbeth?" teachers may ask, "How is it possible for someone like Lady Macbeth to influence her husband's behavior in these ways? What data from the play support your position?"

The Challenge of "Why" Questions Can Be Reduced by Narrowing Their Focus

When teachers strive to use more productive questions, there is a great tendency to fall back on "why" questions. "Why?" or "Why do you think so?" questions come easily to the lips and seem, on the surface, to call for student thinking.

In some instances, "why" questions may be productive, but for the most part, they fail to engage students on the level we had hoped for. For no matter how careful the tone, "Why?" sounds inquisitorial; students feel put on the spot. "Why do you think so?" in most instances causes students to feel defensive. And feeling defensive is not conducive to productive thinking. It is less confrontational to refocus the question or to ask for more information. Rather than "Why?" consider:

- Tell us a bit more about what you mean.
- You may have some data to support that position.
- Perhaps you can give some examples?
- I'm wondering how you figured that out. Can you help me?

Tough Questions Are Made "Softer" by Turning Them into Declarative Statements

It is less threatening to students to hear questions in a gentler, less aggressive form. When questions can be put as requests for more information, students do not have to wade through layers of initial anxiety before offering their ideas.

For example, instead of asking, "What examples can you give me?" the teacher might say, "You may have some examples to support your statements." Another way of reducing the potentially aggressive tone of a question is to put it in less confrontational language. For example, instead of asking, "Is there an inconsistency between those two statements you have just made?" the teacher might say, "Help me to understand. I'm seeing an inconsistency in your two statements. Have I misunderstood you?"

These differences are not so much differences in substance as in tone. Some teachers will prefer the more aggressive questioning mode; others will opt for the softer, less aggressive way. In determining your mode, ask yourself: With these students, what questioning tone is likely to get the better result?

Try Letting Go of the Evaluative Response

One of the necessary conditions for using questions effectively in an interactive dialogue is the teacher's ability to resist the tendency to evaluate each student's response. Teachers have become habituated to using evaluative utterances in almost automatic ways:

- Good idea, Fiona.
- That's interesting Lloyd.
- Not quite on the mark, Justin.

Although some claim that students need evaluative encouragement to stimulate further participation, such responses may cut off further discussion rather than facilitate it (Kohn, 1999).

Try letting go of evaluative responses for one class discussion and then ask students for their perceptions of the experience. Chances are you will find sentiments that match those made by Grade 11 students in the Coquitlam Case Study Project (Adam, 1992):

- *We felt safe to express our own ideas. We felt freer to volunteer our ideas without having to worry about being wrong.*
- *Even if I had a wild idea, I could raise it without worrying that it might be inappropriate. I can be more creative in my thinking and I can stretch my mind in a wider way.*
- *I always felt shy about speaking in class. It took me quite a while before I could feel brave enough to say what I think. But I know the teacher would listen and would not put me down.*
- *Everyone's ideas have value, in some way. It makes me appreciate the ideas of others, even though they are different from mine. We learn to listen to each other, too.*
- *It makes me feel good about my contribution. I feel I have something worthwhile to say and that way my ideas will be heard.*

Letting go of evaluative responses does not mean being unappreciative of students' ideas. But there is a considerable difference in impact between "Good idea, Fiona" and "Thanks for sharing your thinking with us, Fiona."

Conclusion

Learning the "art of questioning" may take some practice for these interactions are more complex than the kinds of responses described in Chapter 6. To listen, to apprehend, to reach for understanding of what a student is saying, and then "play those ideas back in some new form" is more easily acquired. But interposing questions, and the "right" question, at the right time, and in the right way, takes a bit of practice. The most important advice one can get in the process of reaching for mastery is to remember (again) not to be discouraged, not to be impatient, and not to give up. The fumbles we make along the road to mastery are important learning opportunities, and the good news is that there are no penalties for making them – only increased insight into the process.

What I have learned as a student and practitioner of interactive teaching is that there is no greater gift that a teacher can give to students – that is, to listen respectfully, and to inquire thoughtfully and sensitively, into the way a student thinks. When that can be achieved, the discussion that can ensue takes a form that, like making beautiful music, lifts ideas from the dull and humdrum, into what sounds like the harmony in a Bach chorale and fugue.

Key to mastering the interactive skills described is the ability to listen to oneself in the act of interacting with students – to tune in, to hear, to watch, and to learn from this self-study. For it is largely this ability to reflect in and on action that teachers may find the promise of the richness of classroom discussions. We discuss more about the "how" of self-study in Chapter 9.

Note

1 The materials in this chapter have been adapted from the author's PDK Fastback, "Asking the Right Question: The Essence of Teaching." Reprinted with permission of Phi Delta Kappa International, www.pdkintl.org. All rights reserved.

References

Adam, Maureen (1992). *The Responses of Eleventh Graders to Use of Case Method of Instruction in Social Studies*. Unpublished Master's thesis, Faculty of Education, Simon Fraser University, Burnaby, BC.
Bloom, Benjamin (1956). *Taxonomy of Educational Objectives, Handbook I: Cognitive Domain*. New York. McKay.
Carkhuff, Robert R. (2000). *The Art of Helping*. Amherst: Human Resources Press.
Kohn, Alfie (1999). *Punished By Rewards*. Boston: Mariner Books.
Raths, Louis, E., Wassermann, Selma, Jonas, Arthur, & Rothstein, Arnold (1986). *Teaching for Thinking: Theory and Application* (2nd edition). New York: Teachers College Press.
Rowe, Mary Budd (1973). *Teaching Science As Continuous Inquiry*. New York: McGraw Hill.
Stahl, Robert J. (1994). "Using Think Time and Wait Time Skillfully in the Classroom." Bloomington, IN: ERIC Digest.
Wassermann, Selma (2009). *Teaching for Thinking Today*. New York: Teachers College Press.

8
THE WELL-ORCHESTRATED DISCUSSION

For those of us who love teaching, there is much beauty in watching a class in the midst of an interactive discussion. To witness the teacher "in charge" – listening, responding, questioning; the students animated, fully engaged; the energy in the classroom dynamic and alive – is immensely satisfying. To bring students along to this level of active involvement and participation, in which they can trust offering their ideas and allowing the teacher to tap into their thought processes is a wonderful gift that teachers can give. No teacher and no student comes away from such classes unchanged, for the better.

Studying the process, it becomes obvious that the well-balanced, interactive discussion is not made up entirely of a string of questions, no matter how well each meets the criteria for provoking intelligent thought. The construction of good questions is only one measure of effective interactive teaching. The others lie in the teacher's ability to listen, to attend to what the student is saying, and to interpose good questions with other responses that require students to re-examine their ideas. A discussion that consists only of questions will drive the discourse into constantly new channels, without allowing students the time and the opportunity to reflect on what is being said.

For example, the teacher opens the Grade 4 discussion on the Zuni Indians with:

> TEACHER: Tell me what observations you have made about the early ways of life of the Zuni.
>
> STUDENT: Well, they were primarily agricultural.

If the teacher chooses to pose a question at this point – for example, "What other observations have you made about them?" – this question immediately shifts the issue from the re-examination of the student's idea that the Zuni's way of life is agricultural to other aspects of their way of life. To require the student to reflect on the statement, the teacher might respond with:

TEACHER: Tell me more about how being agricultural marked their lives.

By responding directly to the student's statement, the teacher calls for re-examination or re-thinking about the meaning and implications of "an agricultural way of life." This is done for several reasons. First, such a response communicates that the teacher has heard the student's idea. Second, when the idea about "an agricultural way of life" is replayed for the student to re-examine, the student must take responsibility for it. Such attention to students' ideas not only fosters habits of thinking, but also requires students to take ownership of what they are saying. Students are required to think before they speak, to take responsibility for what they say, and they learn that what they say will be heard and subject to scrutiny. Third, it requires the student to reflect on the meaning of "agricultural way of life" and examine what that actually involves and what it means in day-to-day practice. Once this has been explored to the teacher's satisfaction, the teacher can proceed to the question, "What other observations can be made about the way of life of the early Zuni?"

I cannot promise that these responses will bring an end to idle, irresponsible statements, but at the least, it can lead in the right direction.

Teachers who are embarking on a discussion teaching class may want to arm themselves with a few questions in advance that attend to the big ideas that underpin the curriculum experience. The questions might deal with analytical matters (observations of situations, summaries of events, procedures) in which students are asked to observe, to compare, to synthesize, and to summarize. The questions may then move gradually on to more speculative questions, where students are asked to generate new ways of thinking through hypothesizing, evaluating and judging, providing examples, and suggesting alternatives. As the examination on the issues progresses, the questions may call for deeper, more sophisticated examinations. Having a "crib sheet" of the questions that may be used, and keeping it within reach during the discussion, is a helpful strategy to keep the discussion on track, and keep the teacher centered on those big ideas chosen for examination.

In orchestrating an effective interactive discussion, teachers may wish to keep the following in mind:

1. Know the students. This will help to determine what kinds of questions are most likely to be productive for them and which questions draw on a particular student's experiences. It helps to know which kinds of questions are more effective with which students.

    For example: A rather shy and awkward seven-year-old boy was making some observations about mountains and was asked: "How are mountains formed?" His shyness and reluctance to offer ideas made him quiet and unresponsive. When the teacher noticed this, she reframed the question and asked, instead, "Do you have any theories that might explain it?" The question shifted from his being called on to give an answer to being asked to create ideas. To this, he was able to respond: "I think they start as pebbles and grow to become larger and larger, until they are mountains."

2. Know how to listen to what the student is saying. Try to comprehend what is being said. Try to formulate responses that accurately reflect students' ideas.

   For example: Peter, a nine-year-old with a bit of a lisp, told his teacher: "We went to Nassauh for our holidays. We went by train."

   The teacher, listening with only one ear, said, "You can't get to Nassau by train. You have to take a boat."

   Peter insisted. "No, we went by train."

   The teacher also insisted. "You are wrong. You can't get there by train. You HAVE to go by boat or airplane."

   Peter was really telling the teacher that he went to Nashua, New Hampshire, and he did get there by train.

3. Try to respond to a student's statement in a way that calls for the examination of that idea from a fresh perspective.

   For example: The Grade 7 students were making observations of a jar of locusts as part of their studies of insect life. The teacher began by asking: "What observations can you make about these locusts?"

   > LYNNE: This is weird. Their eyes are right here. (Points to the eyes)
   >
   > TEACHER: (Responding by paraphrasing what she said) You see the positioning of the eyes as strange.
   >
   > STUDENT: Yeh. Okay. See, there are the eyes. (Points to the side of the head of the locust)
   >
   > TEACHER: Why do you suppose the have eyes on the side of their heads? (Asks for hypotheses. Much too early for this kind of challenge.) Better response: You're suggesting that their eyes are at the sides of their heads and there's something different about the way the eyes are placed.

4. Choose a follow-up response that takes the student's thinking one step further

   For example: The teacher is conducting an interactive discussion about Pueblo Indian life, based upon a story read in class.

   > TEACHER: Yesterday we read a story about life among the Pueblo Indians long ago. What observations were you able to make about the way they lived?
   >
   > HELEN: They got their food by hunting.
   >
   > TEACHER: One way of getting food was by hunting.
   >
   > HELEN: Yeh they hunted rabbits.

TEACHER: So rabbits were an important source of meat for the Pueblos.

HELEN: Yeh.

TEACHER: I wonder why they didn't just go to the supermarket?

(Pupils giggle)

TEACHER: That seems a little funny to you.

MELVIN: They didn't have supermarkets in those days.

TEACHER: No supermarkets, eh? Hmmmm… I wonder how people could get along without a market where they could shop and get anything they needed?

SARAH: I think it just means, like, you have to grow your own. Like you have to grow your own vegetables and stuff.

TEACHER: So without a market, you would need to grow your own food. And the Pueblos did this?

SARAH: Yeh. They grew corn and stuff.

TEACHER: They had to rely on their skills as farmers in order to get food.

FRANK: Well, they did other things, like collect berries. I don't think they grew the berries, but they just went out there and picked them off the bushes.

TEACHER: Another way of getting food was by gathering what was already growing. There were some foods they didn't have to plant themselves.

(Students voice their agreement)

TEACHER: I guess there's a big difference in your life if you have to depend on hunting, planting, and gathering your own food, rather than just going to the market and getting what you need. I wonder how that could affect your life? Do you have any ideas about that?

5. Decide when the interactive dialogue with one particular student is "finished" and it is time to move to another student.
   For example: You can tell by listening and apprehending if and when the student has no more to add, or if and when the student is beginning to feel under stress during the interactions.

6. Frame questions and responses so that they are respectful, non-threatening and productive.
   For example: The Grade 11 students were discussing Canadian Prime Minister Stephen Harper's "official apology statement" of June 2008:

   Two primary objectives of the residential school system were to remove and isolate children from the influence of their homes, families, traditions and cultures, and to assimilate them into the dominant culture. These objectives were based on the assumption Aboriginal cultures and spiritual beliefs were inferior and unequal. Indeed, some sought, as it was infamously said, "to kill the Indian in the child." Today we recognize that this policy of assimilation was wrong, has caused great harm, and has no place in our country.

The big ideas that the teacher wanted to put under examination were:

- The Canadian government and the Christian churches played a role in forcibly removing First Nations children from their homes, in an attempt to "extinguish" their Indian culture and ease them into the mainstream culture.
- Children attending the residential schools experienced not only poor quality education, but often severe corporal punishment.
- One of the consequences was that children growing up did not know to which group they actually belonged.
- Some of the negative consequences for the children were loss of self-esteem and disempowerment and identity crises, which led later to suicide and alcoholism in adults.
- There was considerable hubris in the assumption that First Nations culture was inferior to the "white" culture.
- That form of discrimination and bigotry exists in our culture today.

TEACHER: What can you tell us about the Indian residential school system in Canada? Who would like to open the discussion?

(Teacher waits)

TEACHER: Yes, Inez?

INEZ: Well, I know that the schools were set up by the Canadian government to take Indian children out of their homes and send them off to where they would learn the values of the white people.

TEACHER: Thanks, Inez, for opening the discussion. Let me see if I understand your idea correctly. The schools were government schools and the First Nations children were taken from their homes, away from their parents, so that they would become assimilated into mainstream Canadian society.

INEZ: Yeh. And I would like to add one more thing. It was a disgusting thing to do. Because the parents and children had no rights to object. They were forced to attend.

TEACHER: Let me try to paraphrase that for you. You see that as unjust and discriminatory.

INEZ: (Nods)

TEACHER: Thanks Inez. What else would you like to add about what you know about the schools?

LUTHER: Well, I know that the schools were set up by the government, but they were run by the churches, so that the children could be indoctrinated into the Christian religions.

TEACHER: There were two parties involved and responsible – the Canadian government and the Christian churches. It was the church people that did the teaching.

LUTHER: Yeh. And what's more – when the children spoke their native language, they were severely punished. And also I read that the quality of their education was very poor.

TEACHER: Not only were the children forced to abandon their ways and their language, they were punished harshly for speaking their native language. To add insult to injury, the teaching was poor.

LUTHER: Yeh.

TEACHER: I wonder, if you can tell me, about the impact of taking the children away from their families, and the forbidding of their language and the poor teaching – I wonder how this would affect the children in the long term? Anyone want to talk about that?

VINCENTE: Well, this is what I think. If you take kids away from their parents, and you disempower them, and try to force them into new ways and new languages, they must grow up to be pretty mixed-up kids.

TEACHER: You see the impact as being pretty destructive on the children.

VINCENTE: Yeh.

PHILIPPA: I think many of the kids grew up without their families, and not knowing who they really were. They were taught that their own culture was bad and had to be rejected. They were taught that the mainstream culture was better. But they really didn't fit anywhere anymore.

TEACHER: They became "non-persons" – no longer belonging to their families and not belonging to the mainstream culture either. How they must have suffered!

(Class becomes quiet for a few moments)

FRANZ: Maybe that explains the high incidence of suicide in these groups.

TEACHER: You are considering, Franz, that there might be a relationship between the way the children were treated and taught and their loss of self-esteem, leading to many suicides. Some people, in retrospect, called this a form of cultural genocide. What are your thoughts about that?

74 The Well-Orchestrated Discussion

7. Know the "right" time to challenge a student's thinking. Know when to shift gears into the territory of the next big idea.

   For example: The Grade 12 students had read a chapter in their textbooks about the beginning of the Crusades in 1095. The teacher focused the discussion on the following big ideas:

   - The main reason for the first crusade, begun by Pope Urban in 1095, was to reunite the two branches of the Christian Church.
   - A secondary reason was to increase the prestige of the Church.

   TEACHER: You've all read the chapter – so who would like to open the discussion? I'd like to ask what you can tell us about the first Crusade.

   (Teacher waits)

   BERNARD: Well, hmmmm – I think that the important thing about the first Crusade was that it was supposed to fight the enemies of the Church – like the Muslims.

   TEACHER: The pope launched the Crusade to fight against the enemies of the Church, like the Muslims. (She holds this important idea in her mind, to return to it with a question later on in the discussion.)

   BERNARD: Yeh. Anyone who wasn't a Christian was an enemy.

   TEACHER: The idea was to murder anyone whose religion was different from Christianity.

   BERNARD: Yeh.

   TEACHER: Thanks, Bernard, for opening the discussion. Anyone else want to comment about the reasons for the Crusade?

   SAMANTHA: The way I read the chapter, it would seem that the people were really aroused. They were keen to go to fight – and I'm wondering whether they were doing that for the sake of spreading the Christian religion or whether it was just a big adventure for them.

   TEACHER: You think that the spreading of the religion was only one part of it; that the knights were aroused because of the sense of adventure it excited.

   SAMANTHA: Yeh. You know how wars are started. People get excited about the thrill of the battles and the adventures. They don't think of the killing and the murder and the awful conditions of the fighting.

   TEACHER: The pope appealed to the people to get out there and carry the cross to the heathens – or be murdered. But they did not foresee what the implications of such a murderous journey would involve. So that is how the pope got so many men to be involved in making that journey across Europe and into the eastern lands.

ANNALIESE: He told them that that was what God wanted them to do. The pope spoke for God. He was God's voice.

TEACHER: So the people who went on the Crusade believed they were carrying out God's command.

ANNALIESE: Yeh.

TEACHER: How, do you suppose, they were so easily persuaded that it was God who was giving them the command to go out and slaughter the non-Christians?

8. Refrain from responding judgmentally to the students' ideas. Avoid statements such as "Good idea," and even, "That's interesting."
9. Work the interactive dialogue so that meanings are searched for, understanding grows, students' thinking about the issues occurs, and students feel safe in telling what they think.

For example: Laura was teaching "The Case of Barry" (see Appendix E) about a sixth-grade boy who was academically challenged, especially in the area of math, to a class of pre-service education students, enrolled in a Teacher Education Program at the local college. The students had read the case in advance and had spent the previous 2 hours of class time working in small groups on the study questions for the case. Today's class would be devoted to the interactive discussion on the important issues of the case. The big ideas on which this case rests are:

- An important part of a teacher's job is working with students who are academically challenged.
- Students who perform at below grade levels often are the butt of the bullying and taunting of others.
- Evaluation methods used to assess student performance are less often valid and more often subject to the biases of the evaluator.

Laura began the discussion by asking for a summary of the key points of the case. Using reflective responses at first to develop thinking about the background issues in the case, she gradually eased into the first higher order question that deals with how a teacher develops strategies for working with underachieving students. This is a transcript of the first few minutes of the interactive discussion.

LAURA: Would someone like to start and give us a summary of the key points of the case? Anyone? (Laura waits)

SEAN: Well this is how I see it. Barry is a Grade 6 boy who has a lot of trouble with numbers. He does OK in reading – but he fails consistently on his math papers. He doesn't seem to be able to add even the simplest number facts – and he's in Grade 6! How did he get there! The other kids make fun of him and call him "retard." She needs to work with Barry on his numbers and she needs to teach the other kids to be respectful.

LAURA: Thanks, Sean, for opening up the case. Would anyone like to add anything to Sean's summary?

PATSY: Yeh. I'd like to add that he's a whiz in sports and I think that's important.

LAURA: You'd like to make sure that his skill in sports is not left out of the picture of Barry.

PATSY: Yeh.

LAURA: Thanks, Patsy. Tell me how you see his performance in math.

RUDI: He doesn't seem to understand the basic facts. He can't even add simple numbers in first-grade addition.

LAURA: He can't do the basic algorithms. Simple addition facts are beyond him.

RUDI: Yeh. How did he get to Grade 6 anyway?

LAURA: (She doesn't respond to Rudi's question about social promotion because she wants to focus the discussion on the big ideas.) Thanks, Rudi. Does anyone want to say anything more about his math work?

KELLY: I'm wondering if he has some kind of mental block against math. You know, some kids just are defeated by numbers – like some kind of word blindness – number blindness.

LAURA: You're trying to make a diagnosis of what Barry's trouble in math is and you are hypothesizing that it could be something to do with a mental block for numbering.

KELLY: Yeh. Because I think that the teacher needs to figure out where the trouble is coming from before she can help him.

LAURA: A teacher working with a student who is a low achiever needs to determine where the problem comes from before she can develop strategies to deal with the problem.

KELLY: Exactly.

LAURA: So how does a teacher go about doing that? Making diagnoses of learning problems? Do you have any hypotheses about how teachers can do that?

* * *

The neophyte discussion leader comes to the class with not a little anxiety about how well he or she is going to be able to fulfill the challenges of leading a productive, effective discussion. While wrestling with one's own anxieties, however, it is helpful to remember that students, too, come with their own apprehensions. Many of them are not accustomed to speaking out in a large group. Many of them have become habituated to being told that their ideas are incorrect. Many of them have learned, the hard way, that a teacher's evaluative comments can sting and be diminishing. So at first, entering a discussion teaching class can be intimidating on both sides of the aisle.

However, experience with the process, for both teacher and students, eases the way. For even if a teacher does not come quite up to his or her own expectations in leading the first few discussions, no one perishes; lives are not at stake. Students and teachers are partners, together, in a new learning experience – where, at first, it is possible that the discussion may not go smoothly. But to persevere, on both sides, means moving forward, becoming more skilled as a discussion leader as students are developing improved habits of thinking. In order to further that goal, it may be helpful at the end of each discussion class to do some inquiring of the students about the process – and in that way, dig more deeply into what has happened, where the strengths lay and what needs to be kept in mind for the next session. These short evaluative talks, at the end, can be extremely fruitful in not only examining the process, becoming aware of why it is important and what the benefits are, but also setting the stage for the next classes.

It is more than likely that the students will provide the data – in terms of not only finding the process more enjoyable, but also pointing to what has been productive for them – that will lead the neophyte discussion leader in becoming more and more the maestro.

9
REFLECTING IN ACTION

One of the keys to successful interactive teaching is learning to watch and listen to yourself in action. This is far easier said than done.

When I began to examine my teacher–student interactions in my "teaching for thinking" interactive discussions, I sat with a group of Grade 5/6 students over a map of Marin County, California, where their school was based. The object of the discussion was for them to observe the map details, and to tell me about their observations. My goal was to help them to sharpen their observations and to raise higher order questions that would enable their further thinking about not only map reading, but also about the area in which they lived. A grant from Sony brought a gigantic (by today's standards) video playback machine, plus a camera mounted on a tripod, operated by a teaching assistant. It was my first time "on camera" and the type of ancient equipment being used to videotape my work is a hint about the era during which this took place. Given that it is now nearly 45 years ago and that I still remember it so vividly is testament to the embarrassment I still feel over that humbling experience.

The camera recorded as I sat with a group of about a dozen students, asking for their observations. The discussion went on for about 20 minutes, at which time we had exhausted the substance, and we shut the camera down. When we played the tape back, the students were delighted to be able to see themselves on film and I watched, listening in dismay, to what was coming out of my mouth.

Instead of responding openly to what the students were saying, I was pushing for the "right answers." Instead of being neutral in tone of voice, I used my voice inflections to lead them to the answers I wanted them to know. Instead of opening their minds, instead of asking them to think their own ideas, I manipulated the questions and responses and tone of voice to shift their thinking to my own. About this, I had no idea – until I saw and listened to the videotape. It was a lesson in humility.

Today's recording equipment is far easier to obtain and use. One doesn't need a grant from Sony, nor a financial outlay of mega bucks to get either a sound recording, or make a YouTube video for classroom observations. Many teachers are more than likely to have such resources in their cell phones already. But that's the easy part. What is difficult is the first look at yourself as a discussion leader. For many teachers find, in what they see, a discrepancy between what they thought they were doing/saying, and what they were actually doing/saying. Lifting oneself up from that initial examination is the first step in moving forward. From years of teaching teachers about teacher–student interactions, I have found that the essential gift that teachers can give themselves in the learning process is forgiveness – the recognition that as one learns, one errs, and moves on to do better the next time, without penalty.

The process of learning to listen to yourself in the act of discussion teaching is very much like learning to listen to yourself in practicing any musical instrument – listening to the wrong notes, the cadences, the nuances, the shading, the smoothness of the melodic line, the quality of the sound being produced. Without such reflection in action, there is little hope of attaining mastery, for how you listen to yourself in the discussion is key to evolving success. From listening, and from discerning the effects on students of what has been said, you learn about what you are doing well and what needs correction. You learn to build in these "edits" in the next discussion. This cumulative building process moves you toward mastery.

Coming to an awareness that one does not become a discussion leader through a "short course" or workshop on interactive teaching is an important aspect of this learning process. In fact, it is a process without end, unlike learning some finite skill, like the multiplication tables – more like learning to play the Bach Preludes and Fugues, which you never stop learning. You never finish studying the art of discussion teaching. Rather than being put off by this awareness, it energizes many teachers to recognize that this learning process is enduring and continual, promising greater and greater rewards for teachers and students. It was Nadja Sonnenberg, the fiery and brilliant concert violinist who said, "Even though I've performed it (the Brahms Violin Concerto) a hundred times, I still spend hours and hours studying it before the next concert, since with each study, I'm always learning something new about my playing and about the music."

One of the more challenging stumbling blocks of the process is a teacher's natural inclination to use defensiveness as a shield against a critical examination of self. For to be more open to one's own experience, to one's own behavior, to one's own style is not a walk in the park. Over the years, we have learned to protect ourselves from seeing our faults – as Rogers (1961) described it, this is organisms' response to experiences which are perceived or anticipated as threatening, incongruent with their existing picture of themselves and their relationship to the world. Rogers goes on to note that as one moves away from the pole of defensiveness toward the pole of openness to experience, one becomes more able to listen to oneself, to experience what is going on within oneself, to be more open to feelings of fear and discouragement – to more fully live the experiences rather than shutting them out of one's awareness (Rogers, 1961, pp. 187–188).

It's Eezier with a Buddy

The five-year-old philosopher, Eli, who wrote his ideas for "noo teechers to member," suggested the following:

> *Sumtims there are no rite answers.*
> *Its eezier with a buddy.*
> *Alwaees smile.*
> *Whan your braen gets hevy, be sher to empte sum and thn play and get sum rest.*
> (Courtesy of Kelli Vogstad's kindergarten class)

Some teachers who embark on the road of developing their skills as discussion leaders find it helpful to enlist the cooperation and collaboration of a co-teacher – someone with whom one has a trusting and collegial relationship. In such a partnership, you can both visit each other's classrooms, comment on what is being observed as each engages in discussion teaching, and perhaps even script the interactive dialogue for later analysis. When two or three teachers can collaborate and work together, this can be enormously additive, as they are able to provide support and help for each other, examine each other's interactive style, as well as join in making plans for further professional development. In fact, in some schools, small groups of teachers have joined in long-term professional development work with an aim toward developing their skills as discussion leaders (Wassermann, 1992).

In using audio or video analysis, the use of a "coding sheet" to examine the interactions used – e.g., the kinds of questions being asked, the sequencing of questions, the amount of teacher talk, the kinds of responses being made, the amount of student talk, the quality of student responses evoked by the questions – can be a helpful tool. An example of this is found in Appendix D (Analyzing Interactions) – and this is offered as a template; it is also possible for teachers to design their own. Any type of grid can be helpful in pointing to the types of questions and responses that have been used in the interactive dialogue.

If there is a single preparatory reading to recommend to teachers who wish to engage in the study of the process, it surely must be C. R. Christensen's "Every Student Teaches and Every Teacher Learns: The Reciprocal Gift of Discussion Teaching" (1991). This significant article describes with insight and profound wisdom the journey of one teacher's mastery of the art of discussion teaching.

The one remaining question of this chapter and this book is whether teachers, who are already overburdened with superhuman tasks within and outside of the classroom, should commit to such a course of study as mastering the skills of interactive teaching. Like the answers to most questions that my students have asked me in the past: it depends. And what it depends on is what teachers see as "teaching" and what is important for them not only in what they do for themselves, but also what they hope to do for their students. To live the examined life as a teacher is not for sissies; but it's the best way I know to make music.

References

Christensen, C. Roland (1991). "Every Student Teaches and Every Teacher Learns: The Reciprocal Gift of Discussion Teaching." In C. Roland Christensen, David Garvin, & Ann Sweet (Eds.). *Education for Judgment: The Artistry of Discussion Leadership.* Boston: Harvard Business School Press (pp. 99–119).

Rogers, Carl (1961). *On Becoming a Person.* Boston: Houghton Mifflin.

Wassermann, Selma (1992). "A Case for Social Studies." *Phi Delta Kappan,* 73(10), 793–801.

APPENDIX A

Practice in Listening, Attending, Paraphrasing, and Being Non-Judgmental

Introduction

In this task the practice of the skills of listening, attending, paraphrasing, and remaining respectfully neutral begins.

Attending involves listening to what the "student" is saying and apprehending the meaning of the message.

Being non-judgmental involves being respectful and attentive, without evaluating or judging, agreeing, or disagreeing with the student's statement or tone of voice.

Use the "student" statements on the practice task to set the stage for the discussions.

Form a trio, in which one plays the role of teacher, one the student, and one the monitor.

If you are the student:

- Choose a statement and express it in a way that communicates a position you hold.
- Respond to the teacher's interactions as naturally as you can.
- Keep the interactions going for at least 5 minutes.
- Participate in a post-session debriefing.

If you are the teacher:

- Listen and attend carefully to what the student is saying.
- Try to apprehend the full meaning of the student's statement.
- Take your time and paraphrase a response that is respectful and non-judgmental, and that accurately reflects the student's statement.

- Keep the session going for at least 5 minutes.
- Participate in a post-session debriefing.

Take turns playing each of the roles and after each set, debrief the session by examining critically what occurred.

Obviously, the more the practitioner can engage in these kinds of trios with different partners, the more insight and skill he or she is likely to develop – before facing a "real" class.

Please note that the statements below are deliberately provocative – since these more easily engage the practitioner on an emotional level – making the condition of remaining neutral a bit more challenging, but good practice for what might be found in a real situation.

Suggested Practice Statements of Teachers Talking to Teachers

1. I don't want to talk about school at lunchtime. I want to talk about anything else but school.
2. I just do my job in the classroom. I'm not getting paid enough to take work home.
3. You know what I thought of that professional development day? Blow in, blow off, and blow out describes it exactly.
4. I just don't like that kid. I tried hard, but I just don't like her. Does a teacher have to like very pupil in the class?
5. I give them a spelling test every Friday. That keeps them properly scared and tells them I mean business.
6. I don't accept any excuses from a 16- or 17-year-old who is late. A kid that age knows well enough how to get here on time.
7. This new reform initiative from the Department of Education will go down the tubes like all the others. How can we have change if the government isn't willing to shell out the bucks needed to retrain the teachers?
8. Ungraded primary classrooms? Didn't we do that many years ago? I'll give this one 2 years before we go back to regular grades again.
9. As a teacher, my first job is to cover the curriculum. That's the teacher's job and that's what I do.
10. Go to an in-service on Saturday? You have got to be kidding.
11. My social studies test? Twenty fill-in-the blank questions asking for names, dates, and places. I've got to see what they know.
12. When a child doesn't understand, it means he wasn't listening. And I have to give him a failing grade. I can't see an alternative to that.
13. Do I take points off for sloppy work? You bet!
14. He wasn't prepared, so I made him write a 250-word essay on why he wasn't prepared. What's wrong with that?

15. I'm too close to retirement to try anything new. I've been teaching this way for 25 years and in 5 more years, I'll be playing golf.
16. Me sarcastic? The kids like that. You have to inject a little humor in your lessons.
17. Marks? My biggest worry is that giving grades is so unfair to the children who try very hard, yet do not meet grade standards.
18. It's hard to know what an effective punishment is. I don't want to be punitive, but they have to learn to listen and obey.
19. Why shouldn't I have a unit on teddy bears? I think it's perfect for Grade 2.
20. I don't believe in a dress code. I think it's silly to spend time talking about what kids should wear.
21. In that class, I do just enough to get by. I've got a life outside of school you know.
22. I'm considering changing my job. The social services in this district are the pits and kids who need help are not getting it.
23. I hadn't realized that school was a dangerous place, until they posted armed guards at each of the entrances.
24. When a kid has been caught dealing drugs, he needs to go directly to jail. The best deterrent is a stiff jail sentence.
25. Read? Who's got time to read! I get my news from the TV.
26. Being in the helping professions means you are really in a position to help others. I like that.
27. Would I lie to help a student? Gee, that's a tough one.
28. I certainly don't agree with the Common Core standards. I think they put undue pressure on kids, on teachers, and on schools.
29. Some parents never come to school when you call for them. It's the ones you need to see the most that never appear.
30. The bottom line of all of this ridiculous standardized testing is that we have lost art and music – and that is a darn shame.

More Suggested Practice Statements of Student Teachers Talking to Teachers

1. I know I was having trouble with keeping the class under control. But these kids are really wild. I've tried every kind of discipline, but they still won't listen to me.
2. How do I get a cell phone out of their hands? They keep on bringing them to school, texting and tweeting, and it's driving me nuts.
3. My principal is very authoritarian. She wants me to do things her way – and how can I, within those constraints, do what I think is best for my kids?
4. What's wrong with coming to school in shorts and a T-shirt when the weather is so warm? Things are pretty informal around here. I think I look OK.
5. I hadn't realized that teaching is so hard – so much to do, and so much work after school. When I get home, I'm exhausted. And then I've got to make my plans and mark papers for tomorrow.

6. I tried everything with Craig. He's just a totally dysfunctional boy. He just won't mind and he won't learn.
7. We've got a lot of tension in this school around racial issues. I'm not sure how to address this, but I know it's important and I want to.
8. We've got a school program about bullying – but that doesn't keep some of the bullies from taunting the more vulnerable kids in the playground. How many guards can you have patrolling and watching?
9. What do you do with a kid whose parents think he's so gifted and who is just really a pain in the you know what?
10. Carla asked if she could see me after school. Here's this young, nubile 15-year-old and she's making eyes at me. I was shocked and worried. I could be in trouble here.
11. He comes to school dirty and hungry. His foster mother doesn't show up for conferences and doesn't respond to phone calls. He brings pornographic pictures to show to the other kids. And he's only seven years old. What do I do with him?
12. I really tried to get the kids to work in groups, but they are too noisy and they keep fooling around. I can't control them in groups. So that's why I have to do all my lessons in lecture mode.
13. I took the papers home and marked them and I did what I thought was right. I put red x's on all the incorrect examples and added the number correct and then put that on the top of the page. When Phyllis got her paper back, she began to cry. But I think that kids have to learn when they are failing, don't you?
14. He's trying very hard, I know. He really is. But his home circumstances are so awful, you wouldn't believe it. So I try to make allowances for him, but that means I'm favoring him and not any of the other children. Is this wrong for me to do?
15. Mrs. Parker came in for a conference about her son, Jules. She is worried that we aren't doing enough to challenge him and that because he is gifted, he should be doing advanced work. How do you tell if a child is gifted? Do you just take his mother's word for it?
16. I gave this great lesson in graphing – at least, I thought it was great. I really prepared in advance and got the kids to do some graphing in groups. I thought it went really well. But after it was over, and I asked the kids what they thought, Chris said she thought it was really boring. How do I respond to that?
17. I don't really understand how to teach fractions. I tried, but I just can't seem to get the kids to understand the basic principles of fractions.
18. The trouble with Jaime is that he's just a mean, lazy boy whose family spoils him rotten. He's a big troublemaker and I really have given up on him.
19. Of course I want the kids to be quiet. How can I get my lessons across if they are not listening to me?

20. It's not my job to be warm and affectionate with kids. I'm the teacher, not the social worker.
21. I don't see myself trying new teaching methods. I like to stick with the way things worked when I was in school.
22. I can't stay after school. I have responsibilities at home.
23. How do I get the kids to think? That's not my job. My job is to teach the curriculum.
24. I've got 25 years in the profession and you'd think they'd think that I knew my job. But now they are giving me worksheets for my kindergarten class. This is beyond anything that I believe in or believe what's right for five-year-olds. I'm ready to retire.

Thirteen More Suggested Practice Statements of Teachers Being Introduced to Discussion Teaching

1. The experts suggest you begin with small group discussions. To me, that means exchanging ignorances.
2. I did my first whole class discussion on the topic of this recent election. And everyone wanted to put their two cents in. There were so many students who wanted to speak. I felt I was losing control.
3. At the end, only five students participated. They are still afraid to voice their ideas and I don't know what to do about that.
4. There's this guy in the group that, once he gets started talking, he never wants to shut up. He talks so much and so fast, I just can't figure out what his main ideas are. So how can I even begin to respond?
5. The only thing they want to know is how I'm going to give grades. Never mind what's important or what they are learning.
6. I need to get some positive affirmation that I'm doing something right. Sometimes, I feel as if I'm dancing in the dark.
7. The funny thing is, when I have a really good discussion, I can't sleep at night for thinking of what was said. And when I have a really awful discussion, I can't sleep at night for thinking of what I should have done better.
8. You have to do a lot of thinking on your feet. And sometimes, I feel as if things are getting away from me and I can't think of the right response or the right question.
9. Aaagghh – there I was trying to stay neutral and not make any judgments, but when Carlos expressed some racist point of view, I just went nuts.
10. How can I be expected to remain neutral when someone says something that is really offensive to me?
11. I know I'm supposed to be learning to listen to myself and using that to help me to improve, but how can I do that in the pressure cooker of the classroom?

12. Sure, I can raise some good higher order questions, but the trick is to keep the discussion focused on the big ideas. It's like juggling seventeen balls in the air — and that is death-defying. So my discussions are all over the place.
13. Is it fair for me to be learning something new, and trying it out on my classes? Aren't they losing something while I'm not doing the right job with them?

A Dozen More Practice Statements Made by Younger Students and Overheard in Real Classrooms

1. We eat protozoa. Because meat has cells and we eat meat, so we eat protozoa.
2. The word dinosaur means terrible lizard. But dinosaurs were not lizards. They were not even close relatives of lizards. So you see, they're not even reptiles.
3. What's this about the Muslims who believe in the sacredness of cows? Cows running loose and being worshipped? Isn't that pretty stupid?
4. What's the point of the class trying to figure those things out by ourselves? It's much easier if you just tell us the way to do it.
5. I don't think it's fair that Mr. Biot's class has no homework and our class has homework.
6. I don't want to sit next to her. She's stupid and she smells bad.
7. The best way to deal with a bully is to gang up on him and beat him up. That will teach him a lesson not to pick on us.
8. Mr. Slattery lets his class use their cell phones during recess time. Why can't we do that too?
9. Heavy things sink and light things float.
10. My mother told me to go to the Dollar Store and when no one was looking, take a bottle of red nail polish and put it in my pocket and bring it home to her.
11. I don't like to come to class because the other kids make fun of me because I can't read so good.
12. I know I deserve a bad mark in social studies. But if I bring a bad mark home, my father is going to murder me.

APPENDIX B

Practice in Listening, Attending, and Responding

Set 1: Listening, Attending, and Responding with Paraphrasing

In this task, you are asked to assume the role of "teacher" in writing responses to each of the statements in which a strong point of view is being expressed. Formulate your response in a way that you think will be helpful to the student in examining the position that he or she has taken. Try to ensure that your response attends thoughtfully and accurately to the idea being expressed. In your response, try to give the student the "verbal material" by which his or her statement can be examined and reflected upon.

1. You know what I think about graduate school? You just collect your credits, give the teacher what she wants, and get out with your degree. It's just my ticket to a salary increase and I'm not pretending it's anything else.
   Your response:
2. Getting a good grade means everything to me. Too much depends on it and I'm not kidding myself about what I have to do to get that grade.
   Your response:
3. I know I'll have to compromise my principles when I take that job. But I need the job and when I get tenure, I can then take some initiatives in doing what I believe.
   Your response:
4. Of course I believe in grades. On the basis of a teacher's grades, you learn who are the stars and who are the losers.
   Your response:
5. Standards of dress are important. You can always tell something about a person by the kind of clothes he or she wears.
   Your response:

6. Everybody cheats a little on their income tax and at customs. It's in your human nature to do that.
   Your response:
7. My friend asked me to write a letter in support of his job application. I'm really torn because I don't believe he is qualified.
   Your response:
8. I know that she bought a term paper for $100 and used it as her term project. If I report it to the prof, I'm a spy. If I don't, well …
   Your response:
9. In choosing an elective, I always look first at the number of requirements. I don't want to take a course where I have to do too much work. After all, I have a life outside of school.
   Your response:
10. I'm thinking of leaving my job, but I'm having a tough time deciding. The pay and benefits are very good, but my boss is very sexist and his remarks about women are very insensitive.
    Your response:

Set 2: Listening, Attending, and Responding with Paraphrasing and Interpreting

Before starting on this task, have a look at the example first, to understand how the dialogue builds.

Student statement: I wanted to apply for a scholarship, but I don't know if my grades are good enough.

Paraphrase: A scholarship would be very helpful to you but it is dependent upon how good your grades are.

Student: Yeh, because if I don't get a scholarship, I'll have to take a part time job and that would mean less time for my course work.

Interpreting: That would be a real hardship for you – to have to work while you are still at school. Perhaps scholarships should depend on need, rather than on grades. (Reads in to students' deeper meaning – takes a risk in taking the statement to new levels.)

1. I've always had my heart set on becoming a pilot. But the course of study is rigorous and it's very hard to get a job even when you qualify.
   Paraphrase:
   How the student might respond:
   Interpreting:
2. Now the scientists have decided that Pluto is not a planet after all.
   Paraphrase:
   How the student might respond:
   Interpreting:

3. If you want to get the salt out of the water, you just boil it.
   Paraphrase:
   How the student might respond:
   Interpreting:
4. Now they're having kindergarten children do worksheets, sitting at their little desks and scribbling away. Kindergarten should be about playing and learning through play.
   Paraphrase:
   How the student might respond:
   Interpreting:
5. I don't know whey they require students in Grade 7 to read Julius Caesar. That's much too hard for kids. It will turn them off Shakespeare forever!
   Paraphrase:
   How the student might respond:
   Interpreting:
6. I don't think university professors really care about good teaching. They are more interested in doing their own research and getting grants.
   Paraphrase:
   How the student might respond:
   Interpreting:
7. I think it takes an enormous amount of devotion and dedication to stay in teaching. There are so many demands on teachers these days, and teaching is about the hardest job there is.
   Paraphrase:
   How the student might respond:
   Interpreting:
8. What's the most important quality for a teacher? I think caring for your students is number one.
   Paraphrase:
   How the student might respond:
   Interpreting:
9. At the Sotheby's auction, a Van Gogh painting sold for 20 million dollars. And that guy never sold a painting in his life, when he was alive. Doesn't that make you mad?
   Paraphrase:
   How the student might respond:
   Interpreting:
10. They only use German Shepherds for search and rescue dogs. Because they are the smartest breed.
    Paraphrase:
    How the student might respond:
    Interpreting:

Now the Fun Begins

Now that you've gotten some practice in working with interactive dialogues in the most comfortable settings, it's time for you to try your wings and work in "live" practice situations. Remembering Segovia's admonition to "never practice your scales more than 5 hours a day," do as many of these practice sessions as is practicable for you – until you feel ready to take on a discussion with your whole class.

Set 3: More Practice in Attending and Paraphrasing, with the Added Dimension of Interpreting

In this task you continue to practice the skills of attending, paraphrasing, and interpreting in role-play simulations. Avoid using any pre-arranged list of responses, so that the situation is as natural as possible. Concentrate on attending, apprehending the meaning, and using paraphrasing and interpreting naturally.

Find two like-minded friends, colleagues, or form a trio. Have each person take turns playing the following roles:

- Teacher: If you are the teacher, concentrate on attending to the student's statements, using paraphrasing, or interpreting responses as you think appropriate. Be respectful. Maintain a neutral position.
- Student: If you are the student, select a statement from the list of "leaders" taken from Practice Tasks I and II above – or create your own issues.
- Monitor: If you are the monitor, use the attached Analyzing Interactions (found in Appendix D) to record the responses being made by the "teacher."

Use your cell phone or any other recording device to record each session. Replay the record of the session, and together code all the "teacher's" interactions on the Analyzing Interactions (see Appendix D). If there are disagreements about how a particular response is to be identified, keep it under discussion until you have agreed on the kind of response it is.

Change roles so that each one has a chance to be the "teacher," and do this task again with another trio if you think you need or would benefit from additional practice at this level.

APPENDIX C

Task Analysis

1. Describe the issue that was being examined in this practice session.
2. Describe your response pattern, i.e., what responses were most frequently used? Least frequently used?
3. To what extent were you able to attend to the speaker's statements?
4. To what extent did your responses stay at the "safer" and less challenging levels?
5. To what extent did your responses move into the more challenging levels?
6. To what extent did your responses capture the meaning of the speaker's statements and give him or her something to "work with" in reflecting on the statement made?
7. To what extent were you able to make the speaker feel safe, respected, and non-defensive?
8. To what extent were you able to avoid offering advice, giving your opinion, agreeing/disagreeing, talking too much?
9. What do you see as some good features of your interactions?
10. What aspects of your interactions need more practice?
11. What new insights did you acquire about your interactions in these practice settings?

APPENDIX D

Analyzing Interactions

I. Responses that attend and call for re-examination of the expressed idea
   a. Saying it back in your own words _____
   b. Paraphrasing _____
   c. Interpreting _____
II. Responses that attend and call for added explanation, e.g., "Say a little more about that, Marvin." _____
III. Responses that attend and that challenge the student by asking for an analysis of the statement, e.g.,
   a. Asking for an example: "Could you give me an example of that?" _____
   b. Asking if assumptions are being made: "I wonder if some assumptions are being made here?" _____
   c. Asking about inconsistencies: "Have I misunderstood you? Are you now taking a different position?" _____
   d. Asking about the origins of the belief: "I'm wondering how you came to that particular view?" _____
   e. Asking for supporting data: "You've probably got some data to back that position up?" _____
   f. Asking about the extent to which the idea is valued: "It seems to me that this is something you care about a lot …" _____
IV. Responses that attend and that challenge by asking the student to project from the statement and generate new ideas, e.g.,
   a. Asking about implications: "I'm wondering what the implications of such a position are?" _____

b. Asking about consequences: "If we were all to accept that belief, what do you see as some consequences?" _____
   c. Asking about the value of that belief: "That opinion seems to be very strongly held. Tell me why you see it as valuable." _____
   d. Asking how the belief is reflected in behavior: "You probably behave in ways that reflect that belief. Could you tell us something about how you do that?" _____
   e. Asking if alternatives have been considered: "You've probably considered some alternatives. I wonder if you can talk about them?" _____
V. Responses that are not helpful in the search for personal meanings
   a. Agreeing or disagreeing with the student's statement _____
   b. Leading student to a particular response _____
   c. Injecting voice inflection that reveals bias _____
   d. Offering a personal opinion _____
   e. Giving advice _____
   f. Talking too much _____
   g. Challenging prematurely, before student has adequately explored the basic issue _____
   h. Challenging harshly and putting student on the defensive _____
   i. The response does not attend accurately to the student's concerns _____

APPENDIX E

Cases

- The Hockey Card (Eileen Hood)
- Germs Are Germs (Arnold & Barnes)
- The Case of Barry (Wassermann)

The Hockey Card

Eileen Hood

"Of course, David, I would be glad to sign your hockey card." In a daze, David handed over his Wayne Gretzky card to the superstar himself. He stood there gaping. Could Wayne Gretzky, the Great One, hero to every red-blooded Canadian boy, really be standing there, in the flesh, no more than a meter away? David took back the card and glanced down at the signature. WAYNE GRETZKY was scrawled across the bottom right-hand corner. He could hardly believe his eyes. He, David Lipowitz, nine-year-old boy in Mrs. Copp's grade four class at Belleview Heights Elementary School, was now the proud owner of a personally autographed Wayne Gretzky hockey card! David couldn't wait to get home and tell Billy.

David and Billy were best friends. They had known each other since kindergarten. Now they were in grade four and very disappointed that they had been put into different classes. David was out in a portable with Mrs. Copp while Billy was inside the school in Mr. Fox's class. Still, they played together every day at recess and lunch, had sleepovers as often as their parents would allow, and were on the same team in the local junior hockey league. In fact hockey was their passion. If they weren't playing hockey, they were watching it on T.V. If they weren't watching it on T.V. they were talking about it. Both boys collected hockey cards and had huge collections which they kept in mint condition. They spent hours poring over the price-lists that were printed in hockey card magazines. They liked to compete with one another for the most valuable hockey card in their collections.

Last season Billy's uncle had taken him to a Canucks practice session at the Coliseum. After the session Pavel Bure had personally signed Billy's Pavel Bure rookie card. David had been green with envy. He would give anything to have a card like that! Since then, every time they took out their collections to add cards, or trade, or price them, David would look at the signed Pavel Bure card with longing. But then, last Saturday, a miracle had happened.

Jerry, an old college friend of David's dad had come to town for the weekend. David's father had bought hockey tickets for Saturday night's game. The Canucks were playing the L.A. Kings. Over dinner, before the game, the conversation naturally turned to hockey.

"So, David," Jerry asked, "who is your favourite hockey player?"

"Wayne Gretzky," replied David without hesitation.

"Wayne Gretzky, of course," repeated Jerry. "Well, here's something that will interest you. Wayne Gretzky's family used to live a few houses down from us. My youngest brother used to play with him all the time."

David couldn't believe his ears. "You KNEW Wayne Gretzky?"

"Yep," Jerry nodded. "He used to come over to our house quite a bit, I think. Of course I was off at university at the time and wasn't home very much."

"You KNEW Wayne Gretzky!" repeated David. This was just too incredible to believe first time round. David began to get excited. "Do you think you could you arrange to meet him after the game tonight? Maybe he would sign my hockey card."

"Oh, David. I don't know about that." Jerry looked doubtful. "It was a long time ago and, as I said, he was my little brother's friend. I really didn't know him that well." But David begged and Jerry finally promised to try to get a message to Wayne Gretzky once they got to the Coliseum.

That night David could hardly concentrate on the game. All he could think about was the possibility of a personally autographed Wayne Gretzky card. Jerry had sent a message to the Kings' dressing room as soon as they had arrived and now David sat in agony, waiting. Finally, during the second period, one of the Coliseum attendants handed Jerry a note. As David waited, scarcely daring to breathe, Jerry read the note.

"Wayne says he'd be pleased to meet with us after the game," Jerry said, looking up. "If we wait outside the dressing room, he can come out for a quick chat before he gets cleaned up."

And that was how it had happened. David had actually met Wayne Gretzky in the flesh and now he had an autographed hockey card to prove it. The next day the two boys pored over that card while David told Billy every detail of the previous evening's events.

"Wouldn't it be great if you could take it to school tomorrow and show everyone?" asked Billy.

"Yeh!" agreed David. "I could take it for 'Sharing'. Aaron Harris would just about flip. I'm so sick of him bragging about his cards and how much this one is worth and that one is worth. This would show him! I'll bet he doesn't have a personally autographed Wayne Gretzky card."

That evening David brought up the subject of taking his Wayne Gretzky card to school the next day.

"Oh, I don't know about that, son," his father had said. "What if you lose it, or it gets stolen? That card is worth a lot of money now and, even more important, it just couldn't be replaced."

"Dad, please!" begged David. "What's the point of having something like this if I can't show it to anyone? I promise I'll take care of it. I'll keep it zipped up in my backpack the whole time I'm in class, I promise!"

"No, David. I really don't think it's a good idea," persisted his father. "It's too risky. Look at what we went through to get that signature. Jerry won't do that for you again."

"Don't you think I know that, Dad? I would never let anything happen to this hockey card. Please!" David was close to tears now. David's father started to soften. He knew how much it meant to David to show his card to all his friends at school.

"Oh, all right, David," relented his father, "but I had better come and get it at lunch time. At least you won't have the card at school all day. It also might be best to ask Mrs. Copp to take care of it for you."

"Thank you! Thank you, Dad!" cried David giving his father a huge bear hug. "Sure I'll ask her." David thought it was best not to tell his father that Mrs. Copp would most likely say no. She had made it quite clear to her students from the beginning that she didn't think it wise to bring anything that was valuable for Sharing. Since she had no place to lock things up, she said she did not want to be responsible for expensive things children brought to school. Still, David thought, he hadn't exactly told a lie. He would ask Mrs. Copp to take care of the card for him, and she might do it. A hockey card would be small enough to fit in her pocket.

The next morning David stood outside his portable classroom in the middle of a crowd of excited and envious children. Lots were from the upper grades and David was enjoying all the attention he was getting from the older boys. He told his story over and over again, while boy after boy admired his autographed card.

Billy stood on the steps watching. He knew he shouldn't be, but he was getting a bit jealous. David was getting a lot of attention. Boy, he'd love to have a chance to share the card with his own class. The card wasn't his but showing it to his classmates would still focus some attention onto him.

Suddenly the nine o'clock bell rang out and kids began making their way to their classrooms. "Hey, David, hang on a minute," called out Billy just as David was climbing the stairs to the cloakroom. "Let me share the hockey card with my class too, O.K.? T.J. hasn't seen it yet and neither has Justin. They'll flip. We have music first thing, so we don't have Sharing 'til second period. I can come and get the card from you on my way back to class. I'll ask Mr. Fox if I can run and give it back as soon as I'm finished."

"I don't know, Billy." David hesitated, "I told my dad I would guard that card with my life."

"I promise I'll be super careful," begged Billy, "Please! I'll only have it for about fifteen minutes and then I'll bring it right back."

"O.K." sighed David. "but you had better not disturb Mrs. Copp twice. When you're finished put the card in my back pack. Put it all the way under my lunch bag and make sure the zipper is done up. O.K.? My peg is the one right here." David pointed to a hook close to the portable's door. David could hear Mrs. Copp taking attendance. "I gotta go. See ya,"

"See ya," Billy replied, running off to his own classroom.

Sharing had been everything David could hope for. The kids that hadn't seen the card before school wanted to look at it now. Everyone had lots of questions for David about meeting Wayne Gretzky. But best of all was the look on Aaron Harris' face. For once Aaron couldn't come up with a "I have a card that's worth..." story that could top this one!

After sharing David went over to Mrs. Copp's desk and told her about the plans he had made with Billy. "That's O.K. David, but are you sure you want to have such a valuable card travelling from one classroom to another?" asked Mrs. Copp. To tell the truth, David wasn't sure at all, but he had promised Billy now and he couldn't go back on his word.

"It'll be O.K. Mrs. Copp," replied David. "Only I was wondering, when Billy brings it back, could you could keep it in your pocket, or something, for safe keeping?"

"I'm sorry David, I don't have any pockets in my clothes today and I have nowhere to lock your card away," replied Mrs. Copp. "Besides, you know how I feel about having expensive things at school. I really wonder if it was a good idea to bring your Wayne Gretzky card at all." There was nothing David could say to any of this. He had known all along that Mrs. Copp was likely to say no. Still, he had promised his dad he would ask and he had asked, hadn't he?

At recess David and Billy met at their usual spot. "How did it go with my Wayne Gretzky card?" asked David.

"Great!" replied Billy. "Nobody could believe that you actually met Wayne Gretsky!"

"And did you put the card back in my backpack?" David went on.

"Of course I did," said Billy, "didn't you see it when you got your snack?"

"No, I had my snack in my desk," answered David. "Did you put it under my lunch bag and zip up the top like I asked you to?" Billy hesitated for a moment. He had been in such a rush to get back to class, he had just tossed the card into the backpack and he really couldn't remember if he had zipped up the bag or not. Probably he had, though, he thought. "Yep!" he replied.

"Well then, it'll be fine. Come on!" yelled David, running toward the field, "It looks like everyone's playing soccer."

David didn't give his hockey card another thought until lunchtime. When the noon bell rang he suddenly realised that his dad would be arriving any minute. He got up to get his lunch bag and hockey card out of his backpack. That was funny, the zipper on the backpack was undone and it was wide open! He put his hand down to the bottom and felt around. Nothing! Panic began to set in as he checked the pocket in the front. Nothing! He turned the backpack upside down and shook it. The only things that fell out were some fluff and old pencil shavings. David couldn't believe it. Billy must have put it in the wrong backpack. He raced over to Billy's class.

"My Wayne Gretzky card isn't in my backpack!" gasped David, trying to catch his breath. "Where did you put it Billy?" There was a note of accusation in David's voice now.

"In your backpack, the blue and black one," replied Billy defensively. "Maybe it fell out when you took out your lunch." The two boys ran back to David's classroom and searched the floor of the cloakroom. Nothing. The whole class searched backpacks and desks and the floor but it didn't help. The card was gone.

David thought he was going to be sick. He knew it was likely he would never have another opportunity to get an autographed card again. What was his father going to say? He would to be there any minute. It wasn't even his fault, thought David. If he hadn't given Billy the card, none of this would have ever happened. Well, Billy was going to have to pay him back.

"This is all your fault, Billy," yelled David. "Now you have to pay me back. You have to give me your Pavel Bure card!"

"It's not my fault someone stole your stupid card," Billy shot back. "I put it in your backpack where it would have been if I had borrowed it or not. I don't owe you anything, and you're not getting my Pavel Bure. It's your fault. You shouldn't have brought the card to school in the first place." The two boys stood there glaring at each other just as David's father appeared in the doorway.

Study Questions

1. In your groups talk about what you think are the main issues or big ideas in this case. Think about each one and then decide which one is most important to you.
2. David and Billy have been friends for a long time. What do you think they like about each other? What do you see as their good points and weak points?
3. As you see it, what are some of the reasons for having Sharing at school? What kinds of things would you say are good to bring for Sharing?
4. David's father and Mrs. Copp did not like David bringing his hockey card to school. What do you see as some of their concerns? What reasons do you think David had for taking his card to school?
5. What do you think of the things David did to make sure his card would be safe at school? What else might he have done?
6. David decided not to tell his father that Mrs. Copp did not look after things for children. Do you see that as a lie? Where would you draw the line between hiding the truth and telling a lie?
7. David wanted Billy to give him his Pavel Bure card. Would this be fair? What do you think?
8. What do you think Billy should do now? Talk about your ideas in your group. What do you think would be the consequences of that action?
9. Have you ever lent something or borrowed something which got lost or broken? What did you do about that?

Germs are Germs

Dee Arnold and Barry Barnes

"Eva, can I borrow your new Body Shop lipstick, please? You know, the bright red one. I've got to look good for Nick," pleaded Leanne. She ran a brush through her long blonde hair and checked the fit of her Guess jeans. In the locker mirror she could see her new peach silk blouse fit perfectly.

"No way. I don't want the germs from your mouth," her friend Eva replied. Eva wasn't taking the same courses Leanne needed to get into university, but their friendship had been strong since eighth grade and the girls still met at Leanne's locker immediately after school. "Let's get out of here and try to beat the rush out of the parking lot," said Eva. "My dad would kill me if anything happened to his new Mustang." Eva earned clothing money at the Popcorn Palace at the mall, and always wore yellow when her dad let her use his yellow convertible. She was also in a hurry so she could check out the boys who paid her so much attention when the roof was down. She tugged down her yellow leather vest as Leanne slammed her locker door and the two girls headed out to the student lot.

"Thanks for taking me to the hospital, Eva." Leanne's smile faded as she thought about her boyfriend. "I hope Nick's feeling better today. He was really wiped last night. He didn't even notice I wasn't wearing lipstick when I kissed him good-bye."

"Well, you always look good anyway, lipstick or not," said Eva, "and you'll feel better when you see Nick. And I'll feel better after I eat. I missed lunch and I'm starved. Okay if we grab a burger on the way?"

"No problem," Leanne replied. She fastened her seatbelt snugly because she was familiar with Eva's driving habits, and the yellow Mustang zipped out of the parking lot. "That Mr. Barnes sure gives us lots of homework for Bi class," muttered Leanne as she shifted the heavy book bag at her feet. "Now we're studying microbes."

"Huh?"

"You know, things that cause diseases and stuff."

"What's to learn? There isn't much you can do to stop getting sick. Those bugs are everywhere, and they'll get you sooner or later. Look at Nick."

"Yah," Leanne was quiet. She knew if Nick was in the hospital for long he would never be able to pass his final exams. He'd missed so much with flu this second semester. "I sure miss having him as my Bi partner. Those labs are hard to do alone."

"He's sure missed a lot of school this year." A horn honked as Eva changed lanes abruptly.

"He was even away on Valentine's Day when I had that single red rose sent to him in Western Civ." Leanne remembered how the rose had faded over the weekend in the office, and the water had turned murky and smelled rank.

"Do you want anything?" Eva asked as she pulled up to the drive through window.

"Just a diet pop, thanks. I'll pay you later."

"One cheeseburger and two diet colas, please. Make that extra cheese, and can I have the meat well done?"

"Why did you say that?" asked Leanne. "Now we'll have to wait 'til they cook it special."

"To kill the viruses," Eva replied. "You're the one taking 'microbes.' Haven't you heard about Hamburger disease? The meat wasn't cooked enough somewhere in the States and a bunch of people got really sick. Some died."

"Hamburger disease is caused by a bacteria, not a virus. Viruses are different. Bacterial diseases can be treated with medicine. Viral diseases can't, I think. I hope Nick's got a bacteria." Leanne thought about what a dirty word virus had become these days.

"Well, I don't want any germs in my stomach," replied Eva.

"Then I guess you're going to give me the cheese off your burger."

An attendant brought their order out with a smile for Eva. "Nice car," he said.

"Thanks," said Eva. As she turned to Leanne she continued, "Why should I give you my cheese?"

"Bacteria are used to make cheese. Some bacteria are good, you know."

"Oh, who cares. Germs are germs!" said Eva as she grabbed the bag and swung the car into the traffic, almost cutting off another driver. There was silence as Eva unwrapped her cheeseburger and handed Leanne her drink.

Quietly Leanne said, "I hate hospitals. The last person I visited in one was my aunt, and she ended up dying. My uncle hasn't been the same since."

"What germ did she have?" Eva asked between mouthfuls of her cheeseburger.

"Oh, it wasn't a disease caused by a germ. It was emphysema."

"I thought germs caused diseases."

"I guess not all diseases." Leanne was silent for a moment before she said, "Gee, I hope Nick is back in his room when I get there. His mom told me the doctor wanted some kind of lab work done this afternoon because he seems to get every bug that goes around."

"Yah, he had to quit the basketball team because he was so tired all the time, didn't he? It was nice the coach let him stay as manager." Eva slurped her soda and downshifted as the hospital parking lot came into sight.

"And we didn't even get to go to the end-of-season party because of another flu bug he caught the day before the party." Leanne looked up. "We're here. Thanks for the ride, Eva. I really appreciate it."

"No problem. I have to go by here to get to the mall anyway. I've got a short shift today and I'm finished at six. Are you sure you don't want me to pick you up?"

"No, thanks. My mom will pick me up on her way home from work. Do I look okay?"

"Yes, even without my lipstick. Say hi to Nick."

"Will do. Thanks again. Gotta run. Bye."

Eva's yellow convertible was out in the traffic before Leanne had hoisted her book bag. She waved and turned toward the hospital entrance. Her thoughts were of Nick again as she fluffed out her hair and smoothed down her silk blouse. For a big, healthy athlete he sure had been sick a lot–flu fatigue, fever, rash. Some nights he had been too tired to go out and they watched videos with his family. Maybe the hospital was really a good thing. Doctors could cure you when you got something serious.

Leanne entered through the automatic doors and immediately remembered how much she hated that hospital smell. The wheelchairs and gurneys in the hall leading to the elevators didn't help her nerves any. Her stomach tightened as the elevator doors slid shut and she pushed four. It was beginning to become a habit, this visiting Nick in the hospital. She wondered about the blood tests. Did they hurt? Did the doctors find something you could take medicine for? Nick was only seventeen. It couldn't be serious.

Study Questions

1. As you see it, what are the major issues in this case?
2. How do you see Eva's understanding of microbes as different from Leanne's?
3. Eva says, "Germs are germs!" What are your thoughts about this statement? Use your knowledge of microbes in your response.
4. This case brings out some of the functions of microbes. What do you see as some of these functions? Add to this list from your own general knowledge, if possible.
5. Both viruses and bacteria are mentioned in this case. From your own knowledge, what do you think are some similarities and differences between them?
6. What do you think might cause Nick's symptoms? Given the data in the case, could you consider Leanne to be at risk in her contacts with Nick? What data support your answer?
7. Given that Leanne has frequent contacts with Nick, how would you explain the fact that she continues to be healthy?
8. Nick's illness is affecting his school and social life. What advice do you have for him? For Leanne?
9. Many people are always healthy while some have been seriously ill for long periods. If you or someone you are close to (family or friend) have had a long-term illness, and you feel comfortable doing so, talk about the nature of the illness and its effects on the patient. Do not name the person. Relate some of your feelings.
10. What other issues does this case raise for you?

The Case of Barry*

Selma Wassermann

"Are you crazy?" my father looked at me as if I had just told him I was planning to become the wife of Tarzan and live in a treehouse in the jungle, dressed in leopard-skin underwear. "No one goes to live in the mountains," he continued his assault. "What will you do there? It's so far from the city!"

His words stung me and I stepped back, looking for support from the oak-paneled door. "Dad," I faltered, "I really need your support here. It's not easy for me to take this job so far away, to be away from the family. But there are no jobs close by. And I do want this chance to be a teacher."

He shrugged his shoulders, for once at a loss for words. I knew he would, in the end, understand. But why was he making it so difficult for me to leave? I was a grown-up person. I was entitled to have a chance to live my own life, to make my own decisions. It would have been nicer, easier, if my decisions were not encumbered by such a family opera!

I would have preferred to find a teaching job closer to home. First year of teaching – I'd have enough turmoil on the job, without being alone in a strange place, far away from friends and loved ones. But as jobs went, this was the only one available for a new teacher in this time of budget cuts and teacher cutbacks. I felt lucky to get it. So what if it were in the mountains, in a small town about 300 miles from the coastal city where my parents lived? I might even get to like it.

Twin Pines School, nestled in a grove of conifers, served the township of San Remo, in what was becoming the most rapid growth area in the state. Drawn by the clean mountain air, the beautiful landscapes, and the low-cost housing, residents found the rural life a refreshing change from the smog and the high-density, high-cost life on the coast. But there was nothing about the school or the beauty of its setting that had prepared me for this first year of teaching. If the scene was serene, life as a teacher at Twin Pines was anything but!

It didn't take many days for me to discover Barry in my group of 26 combined fifth- and sixth-graders. He was a gentle and courteous boy, as if someone had actually taken the trouble to teach him some manners – a pleasant change from the other hell-raisers who made up the male component of the class. On the athletic field, he excelled in virtually every sport offered. During lunch hour, or recess, I liked to watch him shoot baskets, his skill and grace an elegant counterpoint to that rumble-tumble world of unorganized play activity that teachers see

---

* Reprinted by permission of the Publisher. From Selma Wassermann, *Getting Down to Cases: Learning to Teach* with Case Studies, New York: Teachers College Press. Copyright © 1993 by Teachers College, Columbia University. All rights reserved.

twice daily, at the designated hours of recess and lunch. Off the sports field, and in the classroom, he was like a walrus out of water. The grace and skill fell from him, as he wrestled clumsily and unsuccessfully with the demands of the sixth-grade curriculum.

Ever the butt of other children's grim and devastating put-downs, Barry struggled with reading, his pace plodding and his ability to concentrate overpowered by his fierce struggle to decode words. But at least he could achieve some marginal success. Where he distinguished himself as an utter failure was in math. While the other children were making headway into the wonderful world of fractions and decimals, Barry was defeated by simple, basic number facts. Computation was a puzzle to him, and even the sums given to first graders were a total mystery. He was able to make some headway with 2 + 2 = 4, but he was in trouble if the amount of either numeral was increased by a single digit. Two plus three was outside his reach. Forget subtraction.

The other kids did not help. *Retard* was a word frequently tossed in his direction, and even though I made numerous attempts to quell the flood of children's cruelties toward one another, Barry could not help but be further diminished by his classmates' low opinion of his academic performance.

Remembering what I had learned in Education 423: Teaching Strategies in Math, I studied Barry's papers, trying to make sense of the kinds of errors he was making. But the more I studied his errors, the more a pattern eluded me. There seemed to be no pattern to his errors, no consistency to what he knew or did not know. It was as if a different child was turning in the papers each day. If he knew the sum of 2 + 3 on Monday, there was no guarantee that he would do that sum correctly on Tuesday. His responses shifted so radically, I began to think he might just be wildly guessing. On the other hand, maybe the "math chip" in his brain had been rendered dysfunctional. I had heard in my college classes of children who had reading disabilities, but I hadn't heard about children with math disabilities. I tried to remember what I knew about learning-disabled children, but given that he could function, albeit in a marginal way, in reading, I was totally mystified as to what the problem might be.

Mrs. Newhouse, Barry's mother, lost no time in coming to school for a visit. She brought with her the diagnostic assessments made in the educational clinic of the large coastal city where she had taken Barry for an evaluation last year. Barry had been given a battery of tests, and the clinical results seemed to me ambiguous. He was given an individual I.Q. test, and scored 80. I interpreted that to mean "low average." This, in itself, would not explain his math difficulty. He could read and comprehend at a fourth-grade level and he did seem to be making at least some gains in this area, although they were slow. The tests revealed that his math functioning was "poor," but there was no indication of where the problem came from. The report from the clinical psychologist suggested that Barry showed no indication of "psychological problems that might interfere with his learning." The speculation seemed to point in the direction of low IQ as the causative factor, but the professionals at the clinic were better at explaining *what* he couldn't do, rather than *why* he couldn't do those things. Since I already knew *what* he couldn't do, and needed to know more about the *why*, the diagnostic assessments were not very helpful. I began to intuit that maybe there was some physical dysfunction that was outside the scope of the clinic staff's ability to detect. Could there have been a birth defect? Might there be some genetic malfunction? Were there infant or early childhood experiences that put him at risk? Had his mother taken drugs or alcohol during pregnancy? None of these lines of inquiry had been pursued by the clinic staff. And if the educational clinic in the city struck out for me, the resources at the school district level were even less helpful. Diagnostic services at the school and in the county were few and far between. I could make a referral, but it would be months until any information would be forthcoming. And would the results be any more illuminating than what I already knew? I could try it, but meanwhile, Barry was still sitting there in my class, being defeated by the simplest numerical tasks.

Mrs. Newhouse wanted something different from me. She was not concerned with finding out more about Barry's difficulties with his schoolwork. She seemed to have already accepted as a given that he had these academic limitations. What she wanted was some reassurance that this new teacher (me) would be sympathetic to the learning problems of her only son. Would this new teacher work with him, to the best of his ability? Would she see any value in him as a person, outside of his limited academic performance? Would she (me) use his academic failings to further undermine his confidence in himself? Would he, at the end of sixth grade, be more convinced than ever that he was a capital-F Failure, ready for the garbage heap? I looked out of the classroom window to the schoolyard where Barry was waiting for his mother, shooting baskets. Pity, I thought, that basketball could not substitute for math on his report card. Then he would be "gifted" instead of a "retard."

I was touched by Mrs. Newhouse's plight. She cared deeply about her son and was hoping for some magic, something that could happen in sixth grade that would not propel him further down into a sea of hopelessness as a learner. But I didn't want to build up her hopes. I wanted to tell her: "Look here, I'm only a first-year teacher! What do I know about how to help him? Even the professionals at the educational clinic bombed out when it came to pointing to what was wrong! How can I succeed where all his other teachers failed?" I wanted to tell her all of that, but I could only look into her eyes, filling with tears, and assure her that I would do whatever I could. I spent the weekend thinking about Barry. And even though I tried to get him out of my mind, he was never far from my thoughts.

Remembering what I learned in my coursework – that the use of manipulatives in math would increase comprehension as well as skills – I approached the first-grade teacher on Monday morning to ask her for some Cuisenaire rods. This seemed to me to be the right way to begin work with Barry. I sat with him, dumped the rods out on his table, and showed him how he could use the manipulatives as an aid in calculation. He took the rods from me, with a look on his face that told a story, but I could not read it.

I saw him pushing the rods around on his desk as he worked on the math worksheet I had given him, with ten simple addition facts to sum. His paper, however, was no different from those that I had seen before; the pattern of errors that made no sense persisted. I blue-penciled "two correct out of ten" with a heavy heart. The next day when I looked over to Barry's desk I saw that the rods were nowhere in sight. "Where are your rods, Barry?" I asked when I approached him. Barry looked at me, his eyes blazing with open hostility, as he reached into the inner recesses of his desk and drew them out. Three days, three rod-instruction periods, and three worksheets later, we were still at square one.

The following Monday, I decided I'd give it one more try.

"Hey, Barry. Take out the rods and let's do some math."

Slowly, as though he were swimming through glue, he began to extract the bag of rods from his desk. I pulled a chair over to him and got a good look at that cold, hard face. It didn't take many questions to find out the trouble. Cuisenaire rods were for babies. I had publicly humiliated him with my choice of hands-on materials. Never mind that we had used them in my college class in math methods. Everyone at this school knew they were only used in the primary grades. Why didn't I just put a dunce cap on his head and be done with it! Numb with shame, I took the sack of rods from Barry and retreated to a neutral corner where I could assess my losses.

After dinner that evening, I opened a bottle of wine and had two glasses before I sat down to re-think my next moves with Barry. If rods were for babies, I had to find some other manipulatives that would be more appropriate. They needed not just to help him conceptualize numbers, but to restore his dignity. I decided on money.

I put together a bag of coins, about five dollars' worth in pennies, nickels, dimes and quarters and told Barry that this would be his bag of money. "Barry's money," the other kids called it. No one could say that these manipulatives were for babies. He began to use the money as counters. Each day, he and I would put together a group of ten arithmetic examples requiring him to add and subtract money. At the end of the day, he'd turn his worksheet into my "in basket" for marking.

His score of correct responses was fairly consistent, usually three or four out of ten, with five correct being a major event. If there was a consistency about his low score, there was still no discernible consistency to his pattern of errors. Working with him, one-on-one, on a daily basis did not increase his ability to compute or to comprehend these basic numerical concepts in any significant way. In the evenings, at the dining room table where I read students' work with my after-dinner coffee, I tried to think of what I might write on Barry's paper that would not demean him further, that would not destroy the remaining vestiges of confidence that he had in himself. I could not be false and write that his paper was good work because it was not good work; that would have been a lie. If I wrote that, why would he ever trust me again? If I wrote, "You are trying," that, too, could be seen as a reproach. It sounded too much like, "You are trying, but not succeeding." I couldn't think of something to write that would be honest as well as supportive, encouraging and validating.

In a move that no teacher in any education course ever taught me, I picked up my gum eraser and rubbed out a few incorrect digits in Barry's answers. Deviously, I selected a matching pencil, forged his handwriting, and put the correct digits under the examples. Would he know? Would he remember the answers he had put down? Would such a lying, cheating maneuver doom us both? I poured a shot of brandy into my coffee cup, picked up my blue pencil, and wrote, "Hey, Barry. Eight correct today! You are really making some big improvement in your work." I downed the coffee-brandy in a single gulp.

I played out this scenario with Barry for the next few months. Barry, despite extensive one-on-one instruction, practice with his bag of money, and math worksheets, never learned to master computation with increased accuracy. I continued each evening to erase and change his incorrect answers so that I could return his paper with a response that validated Barry-as-person. I never breathed a word of this to anyone in school.

In the early days of spring, three boys from another class came into the after-school disarray of my classroom to hang out and talk with some of my "hangers-on." I heard them talking from where I was putting together a photo display for the bulletin board.

"Who's the dumbest kid in your class?" one of them asked.

Neil looked up from what he was doing and looked over at Mark, who liked me to call him "Bob" and said, shrugging his shoulders, "I don't know."

It would be nice if Barry's story had a happy ending. But the truth is, I left the Twin Pines School at the end of that school year to take a job in the city, near my family and friends. I lost touch with Barry altogether. Did he ever get through his high school with any shred of his self-worth intact, even though he could not do his numbers? Is self-worth a reasonable price to pay for the inability to add and subtract? Maybe a college coach picked him up and gave him a free ride through the academic requirements? Did I do the right thing with Barry, choosing to bolster his feeling of self-worth rather than giving him a correct and earned mark? If I teach for 100 years, I'll never know for sure.

Study Questions

1. What do you see as the key issues in this case? Identify them.
2. What do you make of Barry's performance in math, given the data in the case? What hypotheses can you come up with that might explain his inability to add and subtract simple numbers?
3. What is your opinion of the action taken by the teacher? What risks were involved? What were some potential gains for Barry? For the teacher?
4. What beliefs might this teacher hold that allowed her to take this radical action? What are your thoughts on it?

5. What, in your opinion, is more important: letting a child know that his or her performance is incompetent, or protecting a child's sense of self-worth? Where do you stand on this issue?
6. What action would you have taken if you were this boy's teacher? What beliefs do you hold that would dictate those actions? Can you envision a time when you might have to act in ways that are incompatible with those beliefs?
7. Imagine Barry 10 years later. How might this teacher's actions have influenced his life? Imagine Barry 10 years later, if his teacher had continued to grade his papers accurately. How might this have changed his life? What scenarios can you create?
8. How is a teacher's need to feel success related to students' achievement? How might such needs impact on a teacher's actions? Talk about an incident in your own teaching experience where your own needs to feel successful were tied up with a student's success and how these needs influenced your behavior.
9. In your own teaching experience, were there times when your concerns about marking and grading and protecting a child's feelings of self-worth were in direct conflict? Talk about these times and about how you resolved the conflict. Talk about the beliefs you hold that helped you to resolve the conflict. Talk about the consequences of your actions. Talk about what you would have liked to do but, for whatever reason, were unable to do.

INDEX

abstract questions 58–59
active listening 38, 39
ambiguous questions 59
apprehending 37–43
assumptions 49
attending 37–43, 50, 82–91

big ideas 9–16; generation of curriculum task or investigation and 13–14; identification of 9–11; searching for meaning of 11–13
broad ideas 11–12
Bromley 5

Carkhuff, Robert 38
Case of Barry 104–109
case studies 5, 95–109
clarification 44
class discussions 1–6, 45–46; well-orchestrated 68–77. See also interactive teaching
class preparation 21
client-centered therapy 37–38
closure 17–18
"cold calls" 22
complex questions 55–56
concept development 11
control: maintaining and relinquishing 19–20; need for 7
curriculum plans 9–10
curriculum tasks 13–16

declarative statements 65–66
defensiveness 79–80
discussion questions 1, 2
discussion teaching. *See* interactive teaching
dissonance 6, 17–19

empowerment 8
evaluation methods 23–24
evaluative responses 45–47, 66
Ewing, David 5
expertise 51

"famine" activity 11
films 15–16
follow-up studies 15–16

generalizations 11–12
Germs Are Germs case 101–103
grades 23–24
group leaders 15
group work 14–15, 21–22

Harvard Business School 5–6, 38–39
higher order questions 15, 61–62
hit-and-run questions 59–60
Hockey Card case 96–100
humiliating questions 57

"An Incident in Boston" (Ochoa) 31–33
information: dispensing of 6–7; recall of 64–65; sources of 15–16

Index

interactions, analyzing 93–94
interactive classrooms, example dialogues from 26–36
interactive discussions, well-orchestrated 68–77
interactive skills: listening, attending, apprehending, meaning making 37–43, 82–87; paraphrasing 42, 48, 49, 50, 82–87, 88–91; questioning 52–67; responding, saying back, paraphrasing, interpreting 44–51
interactive teaching: bases for 5; big ideas and 9–16; caveats for teachers on 6–7; choice of 8; dissonance and 17–19; expectations for 23–24; overview of 1–8; positive results of 17; preparation for 17–25; reflecting on 24–25; students and 21–25; teacher's role in 20–21; time for 16
Internet search engines 16
interpersonal communication 37–38
interpreting 48–49, 89–91

knowledge, subject matter 21

Leonard, Herman B. 39, 43
listening skills 37–43, 50, 82–90

magical thinking 52
meaning making 3, 37–43

non-judgmental attitude 45–46, 75, 82–87
novels 15

paraphrasing 42, 48, 49, 50, 82–91
practice statements 83–87
productive questions 60–66

questioning 52–67, 69–70
questions: about interactive teaching process 24–25; abstract 58–59; ambiguous 59; big ideas 9–16; clear 62–63; complex 55–56; as declarative statements 65–66; framing 71–72; higher order 15, 61–62; hit-and-run 59–60; humiliating 57; less-than-productive 58–60; productive 60–66; stupid 54–55; teacher-answered 56–57; trick 57; trivial 58; unproductive 54–57; "why" 52–53

reasoning skills 64–65
reflection 51, 52, 53, 78–81
reflective responses 2

respect 22, 39, 64
responding 44–51, 88–90
Rogers, Carl 37–38, 79–80
role-playing 41, 51
Rowe, Mary Budd 56
Russell, John 5–6

sarcasm 47
"saying back" 48
Schoen, Donald 51
scientific method 5
search engines 16
self-assessment 50–51
self-esteem 7
self-reflection 78–81
simulations 41, 42, 51
small group work 14–15, 21–22
small ideas 12–13
student engagement 4–5, 19
students: conditions that limit thinking of 46–47; control and 19–20; educational goals for 18–19; ideas of 45–46; interactive teaching and 21–25; participation by 21–22; preparation by 21; questioning 52–67, 69–70; responses of 19–20, 22–23, 44–46; teacher responses to 45–50, 66, 68–69, 70–77
stupid questions 54–55
subject knowledge 21

task analysis 92
teacher-answered questions 56–57
teacher-led discussions 3, 24
teachers: control and 7, 19–20; as discussion leaders 4–5, 7, 20–21; as information dispensers 6–7, 20; interactive skills of 37–51; interactive teaching and 6–7, responses of, to students 45–60, 66, 68–77; as role models 39–40; small groups and 22
teaching style 20–21
The Train (film) 26–31
trick questions 57
trivial questions 58
trust 64
Turow, Scott 4

uncertainty 3, 6, 15, 17–18
unproductive questions 54–57

wait time 56–57
"why" questions 52–53, 65
Winchell, Paul 40

CPSIA information can be obtained
at www.ICGtesting.com
Printed in the USA
FSHW01n1357070618
49065FS